PRAISE FOR

HOW TO FAST

"At last! An accessible yet inspirational introduction to one of the most powerful, countercultural, and neglected aspects of prayer. Reward Sibanda is a man who practices what he preaches, through his living (and praying) with a compelling passion for Jesus, alongside a refreshingly relational, down-to-earth love for God's people. I'm grateful for him and for this timely message."

—PETE GREIG, founder of 24-7 Prayer and author of *How to Pray: A Simple Guide for Normal People*

"This amazing resource will be a helpful guide and trusted companion on your fasting journey. Reward will strengthen your resolve, deepen your conviction, and support your desire to seek the Lord with body, soul, and spirit. He puts language to things I've experienced but couldn't articulate—if only I had access to this gem when I began my fasting journey at age seventeen. I will return to this book again and again."

—STACIE WOOD, teaching pastor at Saddleback Church

"I know this book will encourage and fortify you in unexpected ways, drawing you into the intricate ways our body was made to be surrendered to the Holy One through fasting. As you read and practice, this will become not just a spiritual discipline but a place of encounter, embracing the mystery of

God's ways and supernatural outpouring. Reward is the best guide—he's both incredibly astute and he lives this. It is evidenced in the spiritual authority he walks in. *How to Fast* isn't just a how-to guide; it's a companion on your journey deeper into the heart of the Father."

—AMANDA BOWMAN,
director of church activation at World Vision

"Reward Sibanda is a man who brings joy, passion, and a contagious spirit to every conversation. I'm so grateful he has written this book on the spiritual discipline of fasting. It is rich and deep, whether you're exploring fasting for the first time or a seasoned veteran of the practice desiring a fresh look."

—BOB GOFF, author of four *New York Times* bestsellers:
Love Does; Everybody, Always; Dream Big; and *Undistracted*

"Reward Sibanda is a man of great joy and integrity who has been personally and radically shaped by the practice of fasting. His insights are rooted in biblical theology and church history, but, most profoundly, in a life of discipleship to Jesus. In these pages, you'll find deep wisdom, but the greatest gift is that these insights are earthy, grounded—incarnated."

—TYLER STATON, lead pastor of Bridgetown Church and
author of *Searching for Enough; Praying Like Monks,
Living Like Fools;* and *The Familiar Stranger*

"Reward offers us a deep and practical invitation to explore the fullness of the kingdom through his writing. This book offers each of us access to ancient spiritual wisdom and power for today."

—DANIELLE STRICKLAND, author and advocate

"I've known Reward Sibanda for more than a decade. His leadership has transcended cultural boundaries and religious walls. God has uniquely gifted him as a communicator to shepherd his generation, and this book is a timely resource. It's a field manual for anyone looking to grow in intimacy with God and to live in the authority given us through Christ."

—MICHAEL MILLER, author and founder and senior pastor of UPPERROOM

"Reward Sibanda is calling this generation to fast. In an hour when a person's gifts, charisma, and wisdom are elevated, the Holy Spirit calls us to the ancient path of weakness, humility, and depth. By embracing this path, this generation will see the power and glory of God in profound ways. As someone who knows Reward and his wife, I know the truths in this book come from a man who has walked them out in every season. I wholeheartedly endorse this book and even more the author."

—COREY RUSSELL, author and preacher

HOW
TO
FAST

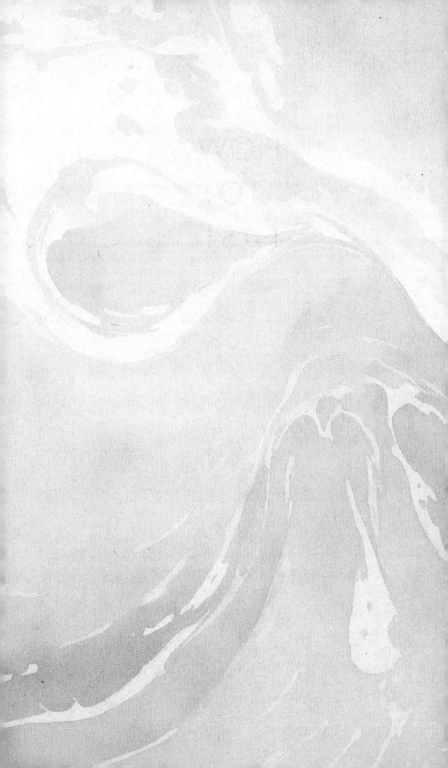

HOW
TO
FAST

Rediscover the Ancient Practice
for Unlocking Physical, Emotional,
and Spiritual Renewal

REWARD SIBANDA

FOREWORD BY JOHN MARK COMER

WATERBROOK

To the Parakletos!
You are an incredible teacher.
Thank You.

To my mother, Mrs. A. Sibanda.
What a legacy.
Ngiyabonga.

To Pam.
Thank you for a lifetime of journeys.

Thus says the Lord:

> Stand in the ways and see,
> And ask for the old paths, where the good way is,
> And walk in it;
> Then you will find rest for your souls.

—Jeremiah 6:16

Foreword

I READ A LOT of books. They say, "Good writers are even better readers." If that maxim were even half true, I would be typing with a Pulitzer Prize on my desk. Sadly, all I see is a pile of more books to read. My reading quota is two books a week (though I work hard to read more), which means How to Fast will be one of more than a hundred books I read this year.

One interpretation of this is that I'm a highly disciplined learner who is devoted to my craft.

Maybe.

Here's another theory: I grew up in a Western culture that was Cartesian to the core. By Cartesian, I mean based on the worldview of René Descartes, the French intellectual who famously said, "I think, therefore I am." Like many philosophers of his era, he called human beings *res cogitans*, or "thinking things," and saw the mind as the primary pathway to change. His work left a deep imprint on Western culture, for good and for ill.

The power of a culture isn't in the answers it gives to the

questions of life as much as *in the questions you never even think to ask.*

I just *assumed* the way to change my life was to learn truth in my mind. So, as a disciple of Jesus with a burning desire to grow and mature to be more *like* Jesus, I assumed the best approach was to cram my mind full of as much truth as it could possibly contain.

Hence, all the books.

The problem is, Jesus and the writers of the library we call the Bible are *not* Cartesian, but *Christian.* While they certainly realize the primacy of the mind in our spiritual formation; they recognize that we are *whole* people, that we are not a brain on legs, but a human being, a *soul.*

Like for my friend Reward, fasting has changed my life. It's become a vital part of my discipleship to Jesus and a key component of my Rule of Life. Honestly, I can't imagine my life without the amplifying power of fasting.

But *unlike* Reward, I did not grow up in a worldview that had any place for fasting. Fasting made no sense; I simply could not fathom approaching spiritual formation not through my mind but through my *stomach.* Read a book? Sure. Listen to a teaching? You got it. But not eat?!

I was shocked to learn (from a book!) that pretty much all followers of Jesus fasted twice a week *for more than a millennium and a half*—on Wednesdays to identify with the day Jesus was betrayed and on Fridays because it was the day He was crucified. This biweekly practice began with the earliest followers of Jesus and lasted a thousand plus years until the Enlightenment (of which Descartes was a key figure), at which point it quietly disappeared. Today it's rare to meet a follower of Jesus who fasts at *all,* much less twice a week.

That is, in the West.

And books on fasting are scarce. To learn about fasting, I had to reach across geography and history to followers of Jesus from other cultures and generations. And what I learned radically altered not just my practice of fasting but my whole life with God.

Reward has been one of my teachers. He carries in his body the memetic imprint of two worlds. He's a Ndebele/Zulu man who lives in Orange County; what more need I say?

This is a deeply good man; his love for God is unfakeable. He carries an atmosphere of contagious joy everywhere he goes. When he enters a room, I feel a smile grace my weary face and my chest rise with a new intake of faith and hope and love.

It is my honor to champion *How to Fast* by Reward Sibanda. Read this book, take notes, talk about it with your friends. But here's what's crucial: Get it out of your head and into your body.

Get it *lived.*

—John Mark Comer

Contents

HOW
TO
FAST

Introduction

Nothing will be impossible for you.

—Jesus, in Matthew 17:20

THE GLOBAL CHURCH USED to be powerful. Especially as we see it in Acts and even the decades after, it was an empire-shaking, change-making force. The apostles and first saints cast out demons, raised the dead, and turned kingdoms on their heads. Yet now such acts of renown are so few and far between. The church may now be able to stand and proudly say, "Silver and gold we now have" (see Acts 3:6), but where is the power?

That is the question Jesus walked into when a boy was brought to Him with a severe lifelong, demonic affliction. Matthew 17:14–20 tells us the father first brought the child to Jesus's entourage with high hopes inspired by the testimonies flooding the region of His miracle record. But those hopes were dashed with the disciples' inability to manifest the power necessary to set the child free.

As the relatively new parent of a healthy, joyful, energy-filled toddler, I can deeply empathize with this father's sense of powerlessness. Inherent in every one of us is the primordial drive to have ready fixes for all things that burden the ones we love. I'm sure his parental pain turned into desperation as he watched the disciples try all and fail.

The father fell to his knees and cried out to Jesus, "Lord, have mercy on my son" (verse 15). Jesus, the source of all power, responded with a moving display of the Father's heart and power and the son was healed. As the good students they were in a shame-averse culture, the disciples approached Jesus by night after their public failure and asked Him, "Why could we not cast [the devil] out?" (verse 19). As an answer, Jesus named their source of powerlessness: unbelief. Not prayerlessness, not hidden sin, not even mitigated spiritual zeal. Simply unbelief. Jesus emphatically called this unbelief faithlessness and perverseness (see verse 17)! Thankfully, He prescribed an antidote: prayer and fasting.

That is where our journey begins.

Prayer and fasting. What a peculiar pairing! Prayer, we get. Everybody prays. People of nearly every religion on the planet recognize and revere the practice, if not the power, of prayer. Prayer is universal, cross-cultural, and cross contextual.

I was recently talking with a researcher for the Barna Group when he mentioned a personal situation he was dealing with. As is the norm in polite Judeo-Christian circles, I automatically said I would keep him in prayer. No conviction, just mere muscle memory and social etiquette.

He chuckled and remarked, "Did you know that 103 percent of people in the world pray?"

We had a good laugh, but his witty reply stuck with me long afterward because the sentiment was indisputable: People everywhere pray, but not everyone prays with power. That, I believe, is the sentiment behind Jesus's indictment of perverseness on the disciples' lack of power. The word *perverse* in that context simply means "common," which is what Jesus meant.

Our philosophy and convictions around prayer are simply common.

Jesus could have used the lesson from the miracle in Matthew 17 to remind His green entourage of the virtues of prayer. I mean, no matter how diligent they were in their devotions, they could not hold a candle to Jesus's prayer habits. He had started His ministry with forty days of consecrated prayer. He regularly prayed all night only to rise the next day and effortlessly walk on water or defy every law of physics by multiplying consumable matter. Twelve leftover baskets of fish and bread—come on, really? There was an undeniable and unmistakable correlation between Jesus's prayer habits and His ministerial potency.

But prayer habits alone weren't Jesus's diagnosis. He went on to say almost nonchalantly, "Nothing will be impossible for you" (verse 20). And right there, He redefined the parameters of possibility. In that simple statement, He made impossibility the birthright of all believers. Through the infallibility of His uttered word, He solved the eternal tension between being sons and daughters of a God who is the source of all power and the vice grip of powerlessness that life often holds us in.

Of course, prayer is the silver bullet, helping us intervene and interface with the divine. Prayer is the balm of the masses.

But prayer coupled with *fasting*—now, *that* completely shatters the paradigm of what is possible.

In that simple formula of prayer plus fasting, Jesus invites us, the church, to step out of the boat of sound reason and rhythm and step into lives of the impossible. This book will delve deeply into how to recapture the wisdom behind the ancient art of fasting.

I believe that the church at large, my generation, and the multitudes of churchgoers have all lost touch with the power of fasting. There are multiple books and countless resources on prayer, but the disproportionate availability of books on the practice of fasting testifies that we've lost connection with something essential to Christianity itself.

Those who have grown up in the Western church have rarely experienced fasting as an integral part of either their culture or their faith expression. But that was not—and is not—always the case for the global church. At the time of this encounter Jesus had with the oppressed boy and his father, fasting was so integral to the Jewish cultural fabric that people rarely had to verbalize its significance. It was a given that fasting accompanied prayer. I believe that is why there is not as much biblical emphasis on the praxis of fasting—it was *that* foundational. In Judaic, Asian, and my own Bantu cultural contexts (among many others), fasting is deeply ingrained, and not just in the spiritual or religious traditions. Fasting is taught alongside other elementary familial and communal life skills.

In Luke 11:1, the disciples make the connection between Jesus's prayer life and His miraculous power, and they ask

Him to teach them how to *pray*. Nowhere in the Canon do we see them asking Him how to *fast*, and so we can surmise that this practice, its benefits, and its virtues were elementary lessons in their cultural and religious contexts. That is why many of the central figures in the Canon fasted.

Moses fasted for forty days and nights twice: when receiving the Ten Commandments, and when interceding for the Israelites after the golden calf incident (see Exodus 34:27–28; Deuteronomy 9:9; Exodus 32).

Elijah fasted for forty days and nights after fleeing Jezebel (see 1 Kings 19:1–8).

David fasted while mourning the deaths of Saul and Jonathan, while his child was sick, and after his adultery with Bathsheba (see 2 Samuel 1:12; 12:16; Psalm 35:13).

Hannah fasted and prayed fervently for a child, and God granted her request with the birth of Samuel (see 1 Samuel 1:7–20).

Jehoshaphat and all Judah fasted when facing imminent invasion from a large army (see 2 Chronicles 20:1–3).

Zechariah the prophet not only fasted but also reset the parameters and philosophy around tokenized fasting for the nation of Israel (see Zechariah 7 and 8).

Esther fasted three days before approaching the king to save her people (see Esther 4:16).

Daniel fasted three weeks while seeking understanding from God and fasted after having a disturbing vision (see Daniel 10:3; 9:3).

Nehemiah fasted, mourned, and prayed over the broken walls of Jerusalem (see Nehemiah 1:4).

Ezra fasted and proclaimed a fast for the people after learning about their disobedience (see Ezra 8:21).

The entire city of Nineveh fasted in repentance after Jonah's preaching (see Jonah 3:5).

Anna, a prophetess and one of my all-time favorite heroines in the Bible, fasted and prayed day and night in the temple throughout her eighty-four years (see Luke 2:37)!

The disciples of John the Baptist fasted as a practice, in contrast to Jesus's disciples (see Luke 5:33).

Paul fasted three days after his encounter with Jesus on the road to Damascus (see Acts 9:3–9).

Apostles and the church in Antioch fasted as they received the mandate to send Saul and Barnabas for the ministry work ahead (see Acts 13:2–3).

Cornelius, a man I deem the forefather of the Gentile out-pouring, fasted and prayed before receiving a vision from God (see Acts 10:30).

Jesus Himself fasted forty days and nights in the wilderness, leading up to His victory over Satan's temptations (see Matthew 4:1–2).

All of Israel—men, women, and children—fasted in times of crisis throughout the ages. This practice was so central to Jewish life that people even fasted for nefarious purposes. Acts 23:12 tells about a murderous sect of Jews who bound themselves to a fasting oath where "they would neither eat nor drink until they had killed Paul." I wonder what happened to them.

It's time for us to return to fasting. Our deviation from this practice has cost us more than we could ever quantify—not just in the potency that could be ours in the realm of answered prayer, nor in the incredible benefits that happen to our bodies and our minds when we fast, but ultimately in the disconnect from a practice so foundational to the faith of our Savior Himself. Is it not time we reached back to our faith fathers' ancient wisdom? Jesus, in the Sermon on the Mount, makes His point on fasting with the word *when*:

When you fast, anoint your head and wash your face, so that you do not appear to men to be fasting, but to your Father who is in the secret place; and your Father who sees in secret will reward you openly. (Matthew 6:17–18)

When you fast, not *if*. My hope is that this book will return a generation to that "when."

Within these pages, may you find not just a comprehensive compendium on all things fasting but also a coherent invitation to step onto fasting's shores with enough knowledge and understanding to dive in headfirst, trusting that the currents of God's goodness and purpose will carry you to realms unimaginable.

Fasting is, at its core, an invitation to intimacy. It's an emptying of all so we can be filled by His all. We will never embark on a fast and come out on the other side empty-handed. It is truly the most holistically transformative experience you could ever undertake. You will never regret it. I pray you will be challenged by this book and that on our mutual journey as friends through its pages, your heart will be moved and the invitation made clear to step into all God's best that lives on through a fasting lifestyle. Congratulations as you take these initial steps on your personal lifelong odyssey of learning how to fast.

1

Body, Soul, and Spirit

I HATE FASTING. AND *hate* is a strong word. Over the years, my hatred for this transformative practice has ebbed and flowed in proportion to my love for food.

Now, I am six foot one, have a somewhat athletic build, and weigh a little more than two hundred pounds. I am not overweight by any means, and that is simply because I love food, not eating. And there is a difference.

Some people love to eat, and the "what" is secondary. The very act of eating is what they enjoy. A friend told me about a Japanese concept called *Kuchisabishii* (pronounced koo-chee-sa-bee-shee), which describes a condition where we eat not out of hunger but rather because our mouths are lonely. If I had to describe my 2020 pandemic experience, it would be that one word, *Kuchisabishii*. And I'm pretty sure the masses are with me on this. The word speaks of periods where the eating is mindless. We fall in love with the *act* of eating.

But I've learned to love the *art* of eating.

A great example of this is in the animated film *Ratatouille* when Ego, a food critic, is questioned by the character Linguini on why he is so thin for somebody who loves food, to which he responds, "I don't *like* food—I *love* it! If I don't love it, I don't swallow."[1] That's me. I love the art of eating. The act is merely a means to that joyful end. We all know the elation of biting into a chicken wing that has the right amount of crunchiness, or the swirl of umami flavor when we slurp a sweet and savory soup. In my book, ice cream should be an extra-creamy, decadent treat. So, if a food lacks any or all the above, is it really worth eating?

What I enjoy more than *what* I eat is *whom* I eat with. Now, *that* is where fasting literally punches me in the gut.

I am originally from Ko Bulawayo in Zimbabwe. I hail from the Ndebele tribe, a rebellious offshoot of the renowned Zulu nation in South Africa. Ndebele are a naturally gregarious and hospitable people, so growing up with an appreciation for good food and great company was literally baked into me. I have carried this formative value into every aspect of my career. A joke I am rather notorious for constantly cracking is that a meeting without food is simply an email!

The woman I married is the exact same way to the tenth power. We met, fell in love, and have prioritized our friendships based on whom we enjoy eating with and hanging out with. That (along with the discomfort of it all) is one of the main reasons why I dislike fasting, and were it not for its life-changing benefits, I would have long abandoned it.

But oh, the benefits. It is truly the most transformational discipline you could ever engage in, and any nation, tribe, or civilization that has embraced it fully has kept it central to their life cadence. Africans have been fasting for millennia. Asians, Middle Easterners, and many others have embraced it for its radical transformation of the entire human being: spirit, soul, and body. Fasting *works,* which is the reason it has become such an irreplaceable part of my holistic health. Spiritually, physically, and psychologically, the discipline works.

*   *   *

In summer 2019, I felt the Lord inviting me into an extended fast. I had done extended fasts before, and I would humbly consider most people in my family line veterans. My mother is from the Lemba tribe, an Afro-Semitic group from Zimbabwe and some parts of South Africa that has a fascinating history and legacy. The tribe members claimed through oral history to be direct descendants of the twelve tribes of Israel and generated much skepticism and scrutiny until multiple DNA tests proved the irrefutable presence of the Cohen modal haplotype (CMH) in their genetics,[2] directly tying them to the Jewish priestly lineage. That sparked fascinating debates, and many books and scholastic journals have been written about the tribe.

Beyond the genetics, the real area of interest within academic communities remains how specific practices and traditions can last thousands of years through generations. The Lemba traditionally observe most of the Jewish customs we read about in the Bible, such as circumcision, adherence to dietary laws, and ceremonial animal slaughter. I bring this up to say that because my mother was raised in the Lemba tradition, a life of fasting was hardwired in her culturally as something done communally and diligently, not as the divine practice we know and have approached it as in this text. Fasting was intended to maintain connection to the spirit realm and keep an optimized physiology.

She then instilled this fasting discipline in her children primarily as a cultural value, before her conversion to the faith, which came much later. So I grew up fasting—not as a unique or even remotely beneficial practice, but because it's simply what we did. It was a chore, and I hated it because my young mind didn't fully grasp the spiritual implications and saw only a systematic starving of my siblings and me. My upbringing was not one of questions and understanding but one of blind obedience and duty, as is typical of most Bantu tribes. So, until I gained what I, on my personal journey, deem my mental emancipation, I used to loathe the dutiful prayer, fasting, and Scripture memorization because we were routinely and daily forced into it.

In hindsight, I now realize what a *gift* those experiences were. When I gained understanding and took personal responsibility for my Christian walk, I found my foundation so solid that the disciplines that take people years to develop in their discipleship to Jesus were already so deeply ingrained in my rule and rhythm of life that it gave me a wonderful advantage. Of all the gold and silver my parents could have left me as an inheritance, my foundation was by far more valuable.

When the Lord called me to a twenty-one-day extended water fast in 2019, it was an automatic, muscle-memory-induced "yes" even though I struggled with the inconvenience of it. I was speaking, preaching, teaching, and going places, and visiting greenrooms fully stocked with goodies was a challenge. But I said yes because I had done it before and knew I could do it. In all candor, there was also an element of guilt, and I felt beholden to the Lord because my only culturally conditioned revelation of fasting was that it was a preparatory practice of sanctification before embarking on divine purpose. I assumed the Lord was wanting to knight me into my itinerant speaking ministry, and I agreed. But I remember feeling a gentle rebuke and redirection from His Spirit, as He brought up James 4:3, which speaks to how people can pray "amiss" (with the wrong motivation). Because I knew (culturally) that prayer and fasting work most potently in tandem, I was prompted to ask, Can people also *fast* amiss?

And that is where the insight that inspired this book was born. The Lord drew me with curiosity to begin what became a devoted, borderline obsessed six-month journey of studying the art of fasting. I studied books and articles, listened to lectures and podcasts, and even borrowed wisdom and praxis from other cultures and their views on fasting. I immediately ran into a couple of challenges: The Christian resources on the art of fasting are truly slim pickings, and the emphasis on most of those resources was usually one of only two things.

The first focus was on the mysticism of fasting, where, like Steve Jobs's initial introduction of the iCloud, "it just works."[3] Don't worry about how—just do it and it works. And as I'm sure you can surmise, the results for those who just shoot for the stars from a cannon of goodwill have always been arbitrary. In most of those cases, fasting is perceived as the humbling mechanism, or the lever that we pull when we want to tug at the heartstrings of God so that He, as a good Father, would somehow be pressured to placate us with whatever we desire, much like a new parent giving in to a toddler's meltdown. The general understanding is, "If fasting moves God, then just do it."

I also found that most of those resources consisted of stories of how different people had fasted and how God had moved on their behalf. Don't get me wrong: I *love* those stories. God used them in my life and journey, and they are, to this day, treasured testaments to the goodness of God, and monuments to the benefits of fasting. But what I was looking for was a one-stop resource to explain not just the philosophy behind fasting but something to make a scriptural, culturally coherent, and historically grounded case for *how* fasting works and how *not* to do it amiss.

The second focus I found in most fasting resources was on the health and dietary benefits of fasting. That fascinated me! I had no idea how profound the physiological and health benefits of fasting were. I nerded out on the bodily processes that fasting produces, and I remember thinking multiple times, *Lord, You're a genius!* We have some amazing Christian resources on healthy fasting from some truly brilliant Christian authors (some quoted in this book). But I noticed that the best resources on the topic were outside the fold, so I had to go straight to the science to find the depth and clarity of explanation I was looking for.

I found that fasting had gained cultural popularity and even became one of the many dietary fads. Brilliant individuals such as Dr. Jason Fung, Dr. Alan Goldhamer, Dr. Valter Longo, Dr. Rhonda Patrick, and Bulletproof's Dave Asprey have seen mainstream attention on the topic of fasting. Ironically enough, although the world embraces the health benefits of fasting, once you add the Bible or Christianity to it and make it a spiritual exercise, the popularity lags. See, the world will always go for the cross without the crown, and biblical fasting forces us to come to terms with our innate dependence and to fight our narcissism. Fasting calls us to die, whereas the zeitgeist calls us to live at the expense of others and forget. In the true subverted model of the kingdom of darkness, the very thing fasting kills is what our generation enthrones, so a devotion to fasting is a declaration of war on culture.

The good news is that we know from the Bible that the desert of fasting is where God often works out our sanctification. Take it from me: You cannot wait to meet the "you" that emerges on the other side of this transformative pilgrimage.

After I scoured the internet, journal articles, and numerous interviews on the health benefits of fasting, I realized that to gain a holistic perspective on fasting with logical and linear actionable steps, I would have to traverse the entire gamut from ancient mysticism and world religions to the realms of science. I collected wisdom, perspectives, and practices so I could be a good steward of this divine call to fast. Little did I know that when I finally felt confident enough to embark on my first extended fast—my first time with the proper knowledge in place—the world would shut down due to the 2020 pandemic and I would be left with a whole house and a whole year ahead of me. You see, my wife was an emergency room nurse at a level-one trauma center at the time and much busier than she had been pre-pandemic, so the Lord used that entire solitary year to turn all my studies into practice, and that's where my devotion to fasting was forged.

My simple encouragement to you is this: If the God who weaves the strands of time into the tapestry of His purpose calls you to a season of consecration, jump in wholeheartedly, as you do not know what the next season will entail.

For us to understand how fasting works and its excellent benefits for our lives, we need to establish a fundamental understanding of the basic makeup of the human being.

Humans are an amalgam of three core parts: the spirit, the soul, and the body. The clearest example of this is in the apostle Paul's first letter to the Thessalonians: "May the God of peace Himself sanctify you completely; and may your whole spirit, soul, and body be preserved blameless at the coming of our Lord Jesus Christ" (5:23).

Paul introduces two concepts that are fundamental to fasting. First is the importance of sanctification, meaning to make holy, set apart, or consecrate. Sanctification is seen as a work of

God, where, through the power and work of the Holy Spirit and our collaboration with His efforts, He purifies and refines our character to be more like Christ. It's not just a spiritual or moral purification; it's a holistic transformation that encompasses the entire person. The process is ongoing throughout the Christian's life, leading toward spiritual maturity and moral integrity and the goal of our being formed into the image and likeness of Christ (see Romans 8:29).

The second concept that Paul presents to us is the tripartite—or three-part—makeup of the human being, which was first explained to me in Sunday school: "We are spirit, we have a soul, and we live in a body." It was told with a catchy earworm of a song we were taught in third grade, and I'm humming it as I write. While an oversimplification, it does capture the gist of the three faculties of human beings. A more mature and accurate descriptor would be to say,

I am spirit, I am soul, and I am body.

As human beings, we are spirit, soul, and body. Understanding that is a game changer and extremely crucial to understanding all aspects of the Christian walk.

In Genesis, the Bible gives a beautiful and elaborate narrative on our origin story and states, "The LORD God formed man of the dust of the ground, and breathed into his nostrils the breath of life; and man became a living soul" (2:7, KJV). He formed man out of the dust (body). Then He breathed His divine breath of life (spirit) into man, and man became a living (soul). God's design was intentional, and each of the three faculties have distinct characteristics and special functions.

Let's go a little deeper.

I AM SPIRIT

In Genesis 1:26, God, who "is Spirit" (John 4:24), speaks within the divine counsel of the Godhead and posits the creation of mankind in His image, after His likeness. If God is Spirit and we are made in His image and after His likeness, we are also spirit.

What is fundamentally true of God's revealed attributes is also true of us. For example, "God is love" (1 John 4:8); therefore, we as humans fundamentally need and will always seek to express love. The object, or the *who* of our affection, may vary, but every human in every context has the inextricable desire, drive, and capacity to love. In the same way, God is Spirit, and therefore we are spirit.

So this faculty is central to our very beings. It is eternal, made in the image of an eternal God.

I was recently reading Walter Martin's book *The Kingdom of the Cults*,[4] his definitive and exhaustive work on world cults and religions, and noticed something interesting: Every religion and philosophy agrees, at least at an elementary level, that death is not the end of life. To me, that communicates a primal awareness that death is merely a liminal doorway to something else, and I believe that understanding comes from the inherent conviction we all have as humans that we are spiritual, eternal, and transcendent beings.

I AM SOUL

The Bible aptly defines the soul as "the seat of the feelings, desires, affections, [and] aversions."[5] I like that.

The soul is what we can refer to as the center of our self-consciousness. This includes the heart, mind, will, emotions, conscience, and volition. When we speak of someone's personality or disposition, we're talking about their soul. Whenever the term *soul* is mentioned, think of the rational, analytical, intellectual, and cerebral part of us. Our powers of deduction are all expressions of the soul. This will be very important as we continue our journey around the practice of fasting.

Because the soul is shaped by the norms, mores, and value systems of our cradling contexts and culture, it's usually a long and ongoing process to align it with God's values. That is why the apostle Paul implores us sincerely with these words:

Do not be conformed to this world [any longer with its superficial values and customs], but be transformed *and* progressively changed [as you mature spiritually] by the renewing of your mind [focusing on godly values and ethical attitudes], so that you may prove [for yourselves] what the will of God is, that which is good and acceptable and perfect [in His plan and purpose for you]. (Romans 12:2, AMP)

I AM BODY

This is the easiest faculty to explain, as it is tangible. The body is one's earth suit: perhaps silky-smooth black hair, blue eyes, and bronze skin. It's the melanin magnificence of a Denzel Washington, or the iconic physique of a Steffi Graf. Our bodies house our spirits and souls and give us agency in the natural realm.

In 1 Corinthians 6:19, Paul likens the body to a temple. Temples are usually bold, imposing structures, and some are even wonderful feats of human engineering. They have a specific ethos and are usually built to inspire awe. Temples are in and of themselves monuments to the predominant attributes of the gods they honor. Most important is that they have physical addresses and people can see and touch them. Yet even though the *form* of temples is architectural, their *function* is primarily spiritual. Temples represent thin spaces where people interface with the divine. In the same way, our bodies are the physical touchpoint where we have the ability to interface with the divine even while shaking hands with our neighbors. All human interaction is a simultaneous collaboration of all three faculties.

●   ●   ●

Our temple metaphor is helpful to illustrate yet another point. Once in a temple, we willingly obey the rules, practice the rites, and observe the rituals. There are lessons we readily learn as we sit at the feet of the sages and curators of those divine spaces. The art of worship, regardless of religion or context, was designed to engage the person holistically: spirit, soul, and *body*.

Romans 10:9–10 gives us a beautiful picture of this: "If you confess with your mouth that Jesus is Lord and believe in your heart that God raised him from the dead, you will be saved. For with the *heart* one believes and is justified, and with the *mouth* one confesses and is saved" (ESV, emphasis added). When a person encounters the saving grace of God, they are convicted by God's Holy Spirit (spirit), make a conscious decision (soul) to accept the saving grace and lordship of Jesus Christ, and then use their *mouth* (body) to confess the truth. It's a visceral and holistic engagement of all faculties in response to the most significant event in an individual's life.

When we better understand our faculties and their unique and significant functions, we can unlock the secret of the interior richness and depth of the Christian life. Our tripartite makeup is the key to our spiritual map of the wisdom and transformation of fasting. Let me explain.

OUR SENSES

As humans, we interface with the world around us though five primary inputs, which we all know as our five senses. We touch, taste, hear, smell, and see. These senses receive data only from stimuli specific to them. For example, fragrant particles will be assimilated only through the nose. In most cases,

misaligning the stimuli and the faculty results in either no perception at all, pain, irritation, or sometimes irreversible dam-
age to the faculty. Imagine what will happen if you spritz Jo
Malone cologne into your eye. You get the point. I have a friend
who went permanently blind in one eye because of an accident
like that. In the same way, if you shine a flashlight into my ear
canal, my body won't respond at all. For proper perception,
the stimulus must match the faculty.

While this principle is undeniably true in the body, it is ir-
refutably true in the spiritual. For practices and disciplines to
work effectively in our spiritual formation, they *must* be aligned
to the right spiritual faculty. Prayer is always a function of the
spirit.

Why is the spirit the faculty for prayer? Remember, God
is Spirit. Jesus's profound revelation in John 4:24 clues us in
to this: "God is Spirit, and those who worship Him must
worship in spirit and in truth." So with God, all intimacy and
communion with Him happen through the faculty of the
spirit.

But fasting is to the soul what prayer is to the spirit. Our
spiritual practices also correspond with this fact. Simply
put,

Prayer = spirit

Fasting = soul

Worship = body

I am a Ndebele man who speaks Ndebele, a dialect of Zulu. Therefore, if you want to connect with me on a deep level, speak my mother tongue. So it is with the spirit. We are spirit beings, God is Spirit, and in order to talk to, commune with, or worship Him, we must engage the apt modality.

Fasting is a different discipline, a different practice, and a different stimulus and therefore needs a different faculty. Let's see what faculty Scripture tells us corresponds with it.

In Psalm 69:10, King David gives us beautiful perspective: "When I wept and humbled my soul with fasting, it became my reproach" (ESV). There it is: The faculty clearly paired with fasting is the *soul*.

Every discipline in our faith pairs with one of the three faculties of the human being. It's absolutely true that fasting affects our whole being, but the primary engagement—the key and the lock—is with the soul. Fasting is a spiritual practice that engages the soul, serves the spirit, and benefits the body, all for the purpose of the sanctification of the whole man in the process of our maturity and growth in conformity to the character of Christ.

With the advent of the internet, social media, and 24-7 news cycles, we are bombarded with far more information than we can process. This constitutes a level of internal noise that robs us of the peace and joy that internal tranquility brings. But internal noise isn't the only combat front in this all-out assault on humanity.

External noise pollution is an increasingly significant issue in urban and industrial areas worldwide. The World Health Organization has identified noise pollution as the second-largest environmental cause of health problems, second only to poor air quality. Exposure to noise levels above fifty-five decibels (which is the noise equivalent of a normal conversation) can significantly increase the risk of heart disease with myriad other maladies linked to noise pollution, including sleep disturbance, hearing loss, stress-related illnesses, high blood pressure, and cognitive impairment among children.[6] This means that even our homes, which are significantly louder than fifty-five decibels, are not places of rest or relaxation from noise.

We cannot escape this destructive cacophony outwardly, it seems.

We are constantly assaulted with the worst types of sensual overloads, and our souls are wearied by all the incessant demands of an attention economy with no end in sight. The Bible's welcome words to the weary soul point us back to the ancient paths—the powerful, introspective, and grounding practices that were given to us from eternity, such as the Sabbath, rest, meditation, gratitude, prayer, and fasting.

This fundamental understanding of the faculties of the spirit, soul, and body became the most revolutionary foundations of knowledge in my faith journey and unlocked the control panel to understanding how the practices the Lord gave us work collaboratively toward the spiritual formation of the whole man. In most faith circles and cultural contexts, this understanding is seen as almost irreverent, but once this simple truth is embraced, our journeys of discovery with God's Holy Spirit take on profound and beautiful dimensions of clarity.

2

A Humbled Soul

GROWING UP IN BULAWAYO, Zimbabwe, I was the eleventh of thirteen children, and, yes, life was chaotic. As a subsistence-farming family, our fortunes rose and fell with the unpredictability of the summer rains, so we never attained a position of financial independence or societal prominence, both of which are important in agrarian cultures. But despite our fiscal shortfalls, we were happy. We were happy because we had a strong faith background but also, and rather ironically, because my father was a no-nonsense disciplinarian. In the Ndebele context, strong discipline is deeply connected to, and interpreted as, love and intention, and by that tough-love metric alone, my father was a true Care Bear. Whenever I tell the woes of my origin stories, my wife (who is formally trained and licensed as an ER nurse) calls him an Intensive Care Bear. It's funny every time.

My father was a farmer and the son of farmers spanning

generations before him. He pursued an education, which was a challenge and quite an achievement in the days of colonial Rhodesia. He worked as a primary-school teacher, which is how he met my mother, who was one of his students. My father was twenty years older than my mother, and theirs is a truly fascinating love story for another book. He worked for a multinational tire company for nearly four decades as a foreman before the farmer's soil called him home. There is an old Ndebele adage, passed down across antiquity and through anonymity, that says, "If you break the ground, plant a seed, and eat its harvest, you will forever be married to it," or, basically, "Once a farmer always a farmer." So, upon his retirement, our family procured land, and my father got busy being fruitful and multiplying his workforce. That is where my story gets grafted into his narrative.

My father was a strong proponent of the "biblical" method of spanking. He would recite Proverbs 13:24—"He who spares his rod hates his son, but he who loves him disciplines him promptly"—in an exaggeratedly pious tone before "doing the Lord's work," as he called it. He was truly an equal-opportunity dispenser of justice, because whenever something had been done wrong and nobody confessed, he would grab the nearest and least fortunate of us and deliver his bespoke brand of African justice on our recalcitrant behinds. When that kid would bemoan how they weren't the culprit, he would respond with, "You may have borne your brother's beating, but you will earn that someday. Consider this an advance." Believe it or not, I tried to bring that up when I was caught red-handed one day, and he cited "interest accrued" and disciplined me all the same. Although his stated motive was love, when he doled out justice, he always seemed to enjoy it a little too much. He passed away a few years ago, and I miss him and, retrospectively, now appreciate his unique perspective and peculiar brand of humor. Fun fact, but when I get to heaven, I will have some choice words for the preacher or Sunday-school teacher who initially shared the "spare the rod" scripture with him.

In my Ubuntu family lineage, there was a tried, tested, and generationally foolproof system of raising a double-digit number of happy children in a harmonious household. The parents poured *everything* they had and knew into raising the first- and second-born children. They spared no expense and withheld no resource to make sure the first and second children were raised to be responsible children with maximum societal contribution. And then they were done. They had fulfilled their parental duties and obligations and were then blameless before God and man. The first- and second-born kids would then turn around and raise children numbers three and four. Children three and four would then turn around and raise five and six, and so forth, while the parents would supervise and adequately discipline from their lofty throne of convenience. Imagine the diluted level of parenting received as child number eleven!

The Ubuntu culture I grew up in offers quite the contrast to American culture and the Western-church culture. When you first meet someone in the United States, after asking the person's name, the next expected question is "What do you do?"

But in an Ubuntu culture, the next question is "Where are you from?" because your communal identity carries more importance than your vocational identity. It's a question to suss out how closely the two of you are connected. A translation of the question in Zulu/Ndebele would be "O wako bani?" which means "*Whose* are you?" And the most direct Ubuntu translation of the question is "Whose *essence* are you of?" with *essence* meaning your value systems, spiritual orientation, familial quirks, and idiosyncrasies. In fact, *essence* is the direct translation of the word *Ubuntu* and encompasses its beautiful meaning. The word *Ubuntu* is a pluralization of the word *umuntu,* or *human,* and literally means "the essence of humanness."

As is typical of most Bantu children raised in an Ubuntu social context, my childhood was a progressive culmination of hand-me-downs—not just clothes and toys but also belief systems and philosophies. That was more formative to me than I could have imagined because when you're brought up in an authoritarian culture and diminished socioeconomic status, you have no social standing and therefore no capacity to develop a cognitive framework that questions what has been provided. I found myself indoctrinated in my beliefs. That is not to say I did not wholeheartedly love or embrace them. I have always had a love for the Lord, His Word, and His worship, but none of my faith was truly my own.

Proverbs 24:10 says, "If you faint in the day of adversity, your strength is small." The most formative practices were merely expressions of our mandatory Christian duty. For example, fasting within my Ndebele and Ubuntu context wasn't just for Christian households but rather was a cultural undertaking in general. Everybody fasted—the religious and the nonreligious. But eventually the fasting was how I stepped off the prodigal's path and onto the way of faith that has led us all to this moment.

At the core of the Ubuntu philosophy is a strong sense of identity rooted in lavish communal contribution. Our value systems and significance metrics are built into this. *Myself* is insignificant apart from *ourselves*. Personal identity is a group project, formed, reinforced, and rewarded within the collective society.

In the West, a person is judged or misjudged and rises or falls on the social ladder solely on the basis of their own merit. The most-prized aspiration and socially rewarded endeavor is to be self-made and wholly independent. A titan! That is the winner's circle of the American dream—the prestigious, exclusive, and ever-so-elusive 1 percent club.

Based on my upbringing, I would describe myself this way: I am the Ndebele ethnic expression of a Zulu man, hailing from a Bantu context. That has been the most challenging part of my emigration and consequent formation as a citizen of this great nation of the United States. It and my formative value systems are not just different; they're foundationally and fundamentally at odds, because in the process of utility, "I" is the enemy and not a comrade of "We."

The first stop on my American journey was a two-year stint

at a Bible seminary in Dallas, whose strict orthopraxy I thrived
under. Upon graduation, however, without my having an
army of RAs (resident assistants) and the communal accountability from a culture that rewards rule following, my faith im-
ploded. As a naturally curious individual, I got thoroughly
and inextricably hooked on my newfound sense of freedom,
and it took me down a three-year explorative walkabout before
I crashed and burned on the party scene. Now, that was not in
the way you may think, as I didn't drink, smoke, or take drugs.
See, sobriety has always been a core value of mine, so while at-
tending college parties nonstop with a girl I was dating at the
time, I acted as the designated driver, in a purely unaltered
state. And after three years of exposure, I woke up one day and
felt completely drained by the repetitiveness and pointlessness
of it all.

At the 2013 TEDGlobal event, author and psychologist
Lesley Hazleton delivered a riveting speech titled "The Doubt
Essential to Faith,"[1] and its premise stuck with me. The essence of her talk was simply that an unchallenged faith was
not worth embracing, and I found that fact to be an important
part of my spiritual growth.

My mind was fried, my emotions were shot, and my whole
soul was weary to the point of despair. That is why the "ancient paths" scripture I shared in the previous chapter, and its
promise of rest for the soul, so deeply resonated with me.

When I hit my rock-bottom moment, I was working con-
struction for my pastor, remodeling repossessed houses for re-
sale during the summers. We would drive to remote parts of

Texas, where he would leave me with a cooler full of Gatorade, sandwich meat, and two loaves of Wonder Bread to work alone for days on end while he worked on another house in that part of the county. At the end of the week, he would come collect me so we could head home and I could take a shower, dress up, jump into the car, and head out to my girlfriend's college town, where we would rinse and repeat the exhausting party cycle.

On that particular day at a repo house, I was exhausted and had a random bass-heavy party playlist on as I worked. The next moment, for whatever reason (which to this day I still believe was divine intervention), a song that was not at all part of that playlist came on. The song—"In the Presence of Jehovah" by Geron Davis[2]—was cemented in my core memories because it was the song that had played when I had the most beautiful encounter with the Lord at a small prayer group. In pre-algorithm days, that song inexplicably started playing. This triggered a visceral reminder of the overwhelming peace, sublime joy, extreme happiness, and unquestionable love that I had always found in the presence of God. As in the parable of the prodigal son, I "came to myself" (see Luke 15:17) and broke down in tears as the Lord led me back to Him. After that, I called a woman I knew had been relentlessly praying for me, and she just happened to be at a Wednesday night Bible study less than thirty minutes away. I dropped everything, got in my car, and drove there, bawling the whole way. I walked into the Bible study, completely covered in paint, with zero regard for my physical appearance, and just fell into her arms sobbing. I was exhausted, and the atmosphere was so healing and welcoming that I didn't care who was watching or what I looked like. I was home, I was done, and I was undone. The woman prayed for me, encouraged me, and introduced me to the pastor of that church. He was an African pastor of Nigerian descent and exhibited the type of redemptive authority I needed in that moment. He looked me in the eyes and said, "You are done with that life. I want you to consecrate yourself with a three-day fast starting tomorrow."

I was so desperate, broken, and happy to have found a sense of home that I told him, "I'll start right now."

A teacher by training, he asked me if I had any questions for him about how to fast the right way. I told him no as my conditioning of never questioning authority kicked in. He then said something that birthed a voracious student in me and completely changed how I engaged the Bible. In his thick Nigerian accent, which always seemed to make everything he said profound, he told me, "Young man, you seem intelligent, so never just take anyone's word for anything in the Bible without asking how it works. Questions are the lifeline of our faith. Blind obedience is how people create cults. Ask questions so you can follow well, because when you follow well, you leave a clear path for the ones coming after you."

Those simple yet profound words marked me deeply and turned me into a "noble" individual (Acts 17:11, NIV), as the apostle Paul called the curious and studious recipients of his teachings in Berea.

It is my intention now to give you this framework so that

words like *what, how, who, when,* and *why* become indispensable tools on your journey into the art and practice of fasting.

＊　＊　＊

In the preceding chapter, we established that the fasting practice directly interfaces with the faculty of the soul. Now it's time for us to go in depth and understand exactly *how* that happens.

The verse mentioned in that chapter gives us a key insight: "I wept and humbled my soul with fasting" (Psalm 69:10, ESV). We see the word *humbled* used here and in other references too (see 35:13). And Ezra 8:21 says, "I proclaimed a fast there at the river Ahava, that we might *humble* ourselves before our God, to seek from Him the right way for us and our little ones and all our possessions."

A very peculiar narrative is in the story of Ahab. First Kings 21:25–26 tells us, "There was no one like Ahab who sold himself to do wickedness in the sight of the LORD, because Jezebel his wife stirred him up. And he behaved very abominably in following idols." Ahab literally gets the uncoveted honor of being the most deplorable human to ever exist. His unholy union with the notorious Jezebel roped him into a plot (that coincidentally involved setting a trap by faking a fast) that ended in murder. That tipped the scales of the Lord's wrath and judgment, and He sent the prophet Elijah to announce the divine verdict and the utter annihilation of Ahab's entire bloodline. Ahab responded in an extremely uncharacteristic way. Verse 27 states, "So it was, when Ahab heard those words, that he tore his clothes and put sackcloth on his body, and fasted and lay in sackcloth, and went about mourning." Perhaps from cowardice (which is typical of men of vice and avarice), an acute sense of self-preservation, or maybe even a place of genuine repentance, Ahab rended his robes and prostrated himself before the Lord and *fasted*! And God received his fast: "The word of the LORD came to Elijah the Tishbite, saying, 'See how Ahab has *humbled* himself before Me? Because he has *humbled* himself before Me, I will not bring the calamity in his days'" (verses 28–29).

Ahab humbled his soul, and that simple action of humility in the eyes and scales of heaven was a greater weight than the cumulation of his murders, idolatry, and debauchery, so the Lord granted a stay of execution. Fasting when used with prayer is unstoppable, but even the most ill-intentioned act of fasting from the most unworthy source garners the attention of heaven.

Fasting humbles the soul, and if you get nothing else from this book, that is the key revelation that should incentivize you to not just frequently engage with this practice but also center your life around it. There are many incredible benefits to a fasted soul, and we will delve into all of them, but the primary one can be understood, and consequently enjoyed, only within the context of prayer. The primary incentive for *why* we should fast is that when used correctly (in tandem and partnership with prayer), it makes the impossible possible. This lofty and provocative promise comes directly from the lips of the Master: "Nothing will be impossible for you" (Matthew 17:20).

Our Lord said it best in the Sermon on the Mount:

When you fast, do not be like the hypocrites, with a sad countenance. For they disfigure their faces that they may appear to men to be fasting. Assuredly I say to you, they have their reward. But you, when you fast, anoint your head and wash your face, so that you do not appear to men to be fasting, but to your Father who is in the secret place; and your Father who sees in secret shall reward you openly. (Matthew 6:16–18)

Planted on the infallibility of God's Word and the immutability of His promise, fasting truly has a reward. And the Lord promises us an open one. Even with the public reward being mentioned here, I have found that the most lasting and transformational benefit to fasting is the gift of humility.

Humility is that virtue that, in every culture and context, is the brand of the mature. In Ubuntu culture, the belief is that every social interaction is a communal space. If someone in the conversation begins boasting or talking excessively about themselves, they end up taking up too much space, which would mean the other person has to diminish their contribution to maintain social or spatial equilibrium. A friend of mine, Rabbi Jason Sobel, mentioned a similar understanding within Jewish culture. He defined *humility* as taking the right amount of space in a room.

The very basis of our faith speaks to a creation constantly humbling itself in the presence of a holy God. Humility is always the bedrock of worship.

When you fast, your soul is effectively humbled, but you

cannot fast yourself into the character of humility. That is a result of a life submitted to the leadership and direction of the Lord and His Spirit. Fasting humbles your soul so your spirit can pray, and there, in that rare and beautiful space, Jesus meets you to form and renew you.

3

Making the Impossible Possible

LET ME POSE A hypothesis to you. If you knew beyond the shadow of any doubt that the arc of heaven's will bent toward your prayers, would you pray more or less? What type of prayers would you pray? The phenomenal news I have for you today is that Jesus, without reservation, clearly states that to be the case. There is a place in prayer where, to state it again, "nothing will be impossible for you" (Matthew 17:20). And that place is in the combination of prayer and fasting.

We know that fasting humbles the soul. That truth is the linchpin and the secret to powerful prayer: "Confess your trespasses to one another, and pray for one another, that you may be healed. The effective, fervent prayer of a righteous man avails much" (James 5:16).

That scripture captures the caliber of prayer we should all aspire to, doesn't it? It implies a prayer that is active, impactful, and filled with power. The big question then becomes, how does this seemingly simple act of fasting unlock the profound potency where impossibility becomes our norm?

We have established that the spirit, which is the part of the tripartite man that comes from and communicates with God, is the primary engagement faculty when it comes to prayer. This faculty (the spirit) has no issue at all being convinced of the impossible becoming possible, because it emanates from the spiritual realm, the realm of impossibilities. All the things we pray and petition for here on earth—all wonders and miracles—are commonplace occurrences in heaven's realm. Our super is their natural. So it follows that whenever we pray in the faculty of the spirit, there is no interference, no resistance, no hesitance.

In the same way, I believe the prayer of faith that James talks about is one that rises from and is anchored to the promises of God, Spirit to spirit: "The prayer of faith will save the sick, and the Lord will raise him up. And if he has committed sins, he will be forgiven" (verse 15).

When we pray in faith and when the spirit is in ascendance, it's a direct, uninterrupted, static-free line to a God who is willing—and, in fact, desires—to give us good things. For the spirit to be in a state of ascendancy, something else must be in a place of subservience, and that is the soul.

Remember, the soul is the rational you and, at least while anchored in this broken world, is antithetical to things of the spirit, because things of the spirit are not logical or tangible and therefore cannot be explained rationally. We have all seen that. Whenever we are prompted to pray the prayer of faith,

maybe in praying for a healing miracle or restoration in a frac-
tured relationship, the moment we begin to engage in prayer,
the mind (which is part of the soul) instinctively goes into
overdrive to make a logical case as to why the things we are
asking for are impossible. And it seems the stronger that voice
gets, the weaker our faith conviction becomes. Our senses, our
memories, and historic and scientific fact, along with our fears
of embarrassment and rejection, immediately build a bulletproof case for why our appeals to the divine are not practical,
not justified, not warranted, and will never materialize. We all
have, in those moments, felt the doubt rise and coagulate into
unbelief, and right then, we fail to ask boldly, confidently, fear-
lessly, or in a state of any of the divinely prescribed synonyms
that make the prayer of faith a guarantee.

What happens internally is that our souls are in a place of
ascendancy, and our spirits are in a state of subservience, and
as long as that is the dynamic, differential, or status quo, we are
what the Bible calls "a double-minded man, unstable in all his
ways" (James 1:8) and unable to receive anything from the
Lord (see verse 7).

I know I echo the frustrated sighs of billions who experience
that sad state. If only there were something—a spiritual tool,
an ancient practice—that could recalibrate the imbalance and
put things right side up. If only there were something that
could tame and humble the soul.

There's an old story about a gambling man who had two
dogs he would race, and with startling accuracy, he could pre-
dict which dog would win the race that day. Upon his retirement from his lucrative enterprise, people asked him the secret

of his accurate predictions, and he said, "Oh, I would alternate feedings on the morning of the race, and whichever dog I fed won the race." What we feed gets stronger, and what is stronger dominates. So is the case with the spirit and the soul: Whatever is fed rises to ascendancy and we glean the fruit of that faculty, whether faith or unbelief.

Paul, in his letter to the Galatians, puts it this way: "Do not be deceived, God is not mocked; for whatever a man sows, that he will also reap. For he who sows to his flesh will of the flesh reap corruption, but he who sows to the Spirit will of the Spirit reap everlasting life" (6:7–8).

Now, in that and a few other contexts, Paul and other New Testament authors use that term *the flesh*. Even though most people take the flesh to mean the physical body, deeper study proves that it is much more than that. The flesh has works (see 5:19–21) and desires and cravings (see Ephesians 2:3).

In those verses (and the many others throughout Scripture), the whole disposition of the flesh is almost always expressed in contrast to, and even as antagonistic to, the spirit. First Peter 2:11 tells us, "Dear friends, I urge you, as foreigners and exiles, to abstain from sinful desires, which wage war against your soul" (NIV). There is an internal war being waged between faculties.

Please don't look at those scriptures and envision a permanent divide within our tripartite makeup. Rather, they specifically refer to the ongoing struggle within all Christians between the renewed nature, which desires God, and our sinful nature, which seeks expression in contrary directions.

In most cases, that dynamic between the soul and the flesh

is the root of many issues with our humanity. But through the process of sanctification, Christ brings our whole beings into harmony on the journey of becoming Christlike. First Thessalonians 5:23 says, "May the God of peace Himself sanctify you completely; and may your whole spirit, soul, and body be preserved blameless at the coming of our Lord Jesus Christ." It is interesting to note that the body itself undergoes its own transformation process, as we shall see in upcoming chapters.

A prideful soul, in ascendancy over the spirit, is prone to unbelief, and unbelief is an ironclad guarantee for unanswered prayer. That is why Jesus, when explaining the cause of the disciples' inability to heal the boy in Matthew 17:14–21, spoke to the perversity of their unbelief and landed His whole discourse with this statement: "This kind does not go out except by prayer and fasting" (verse 21).

Of the myriad benefits the Lord gives us through our fasting, I believe humility is the most important. Fasting humbles our soul so our spirits can truly connect with God and His Spirit. We've all experienced moments when we failed to connect with the peace and calm of the reassurances of God's presence and His promises simply because we were too close to the problem—too rattled, distracted, or distraught. A soul humbled through fasting does away with all that. Think of fasting as an anchor for our minds and our emotions for the times when we have no faith, conviction, or cognitive clarity to pray. Fasting negates the paralyzing power of our brains overriding what our spirits know to be true.

THE MYTH OF FASTING POWER

A mistake that I've seen well-intentioned preachers and teachers make, which I believe has been the weakest link to our living and moving in this realm of impossibilities and answered prayers, is that they inadvertently read Jesus's statement in Matthew 17:21 to mean "This kind of *demon* does not go out except by prayer and fasting." The use of "does not go out" is consistent with exorcism language and so has added to that assumption. But that misconception is really dangerous because it sets up a pseudo-premise where people believe, *The more I fast and pray, the more powerful I get in the spirit.* And that sounds good to us and resonates with our reasoning because that is how the world and the kingdom of darkness works.

Every superhero movie or show with a supernatural premise always hinges its narrative on the idea that the more one trains, grows, and engages in a specific activity, the more powerful one gets. But that could not be further from the truth in the way of Christ. That mired belief merely drags us away from the finished work of Jesus and leads to a works-based meritocracy where we "earn" influence and authority in the spirit. The beauty of the Tetelestai (or of Jesus saying, "It is finished!" [John 19:30]) on the cross is the simple fact that from that moment on, any interfacing with all things good and spiritual flow through *His* power and *His* grace. Our works cannot and will never add an ounce of power to His finished work or the authority of His name. Only God can satisfy God's demands,[1] and the full demand of God is met only in Christ

Jesus. If not clarified, the dangerous result of that misunderstanding is that people presume, *The thing I prayed for didn't happen, my metaphorical mountain didn't move, so I must not have prayed enough.* Even on our best days, our works will always fall short of the glory and grace of God, and if used as the currency to get anything from Him, no matter how nobly intentioned our works may be, they will become idols that will always fail us in the end. Jesus, in that statement, meant something else entirely, and to understand His nuanced meaning in that verse, we need to notice that the subject has shifted:

The disciples ask, "Why could we not cast [the demon] out?" (Matthew 17:19). The demon is the subject here.

And Jesus responds, "Because of your unbelief" (verse 20). Jesus shifts the subject to their *unbelief*.

Demons do not obey us because we have saved up power though fasting and praying, as if this were some video game and we collected authority like experience points; they obey us because we extend the influence and scepter of God's kingdom authority that we are under, and it is God's authority they obey. Anything we do in the kingdom based on our own ability will ebb and flow based on our own holiness. The consistency in potency and result comes only because the works were finished on the cross and in eternity. God, our Father, brings us in through the blood of Jesus, puts His robe of righteousness on us, gives us the ring of His authority, and allows us to conduct kingdom business on earth, which includes evicting, or casting out, the illegal occupants of a lesser kingdom from our heads, hearts, and homes.

That is why a humbled soul is so crucial. In Matthew 17, the disciples easily could have looked at the boy, heard his father tell stories of the child's past manifestations, and maybe even known of tried-and-true methods that had failed to bring respite. Based on all the data input, they crunched the numbers in their minds (a faculty of the soul) and came up with a list of all the *logical* reasons the feat was impossible. The rest was history. They could not pray in faith or command in faith, because in that moment, their spirits were in a place of subservience, and their souls reigned unchallenged.

Look at every moment when Jesus was frustrated with the disciples for not doing something He expected them to be able to do and you'll see He always reprimanded them with the same indictment: "O you of little faith."[2]

Faith—the nonnegotiable to a life of the impossible and a true prerequisite for us as we extend the influence of God's kingdom over the earth—can exist only in its pure, miracle-working capacity in a tripartite being who is rightly aligned with their spirit in a place of ascendancy over the soul. And the God who hears promises to respond:

> These things I have written to you who believe in the name of the Son of God, that you may know that you have eternal life, and that you may continue to believe in the name of the Son of God.

Now this is the confidence that we have in Him, that if we ask anything according to His will, He hears us. And if we know that He hears us, whatever we ask, we know that we have the petitions that we have asked of Him. (1 John 5:13–15)

The impossible becoming inconsequential to us—that is the promised open reward of prayer. Once our souls are humbled through fasting, we are finally positioned to begin the serious and joyous kingdom work God has laid before us to do.

4

Foundations

IN MOST ANCIENT CONTEXTS, cultures, and religions, fasting is viewed as abstinence from all food. That is what we call "water fasting." A comprehensive study will show that whenever the Bible mentions fasting, unless specified otherwise, it's referring to water fasting. Let's dive into why water fasting is the primary fasting model God prescribed for us.

There are, of course, other fasts out there, the most notable being the Fast of Daniel. Some people champion fasts from social media and specific entertainment. Although moderation, or outright cessation, of indulgent habits is beneficial, those acts are not consistent with the biblical form of fasting and therefore cannot be used as substitutes for it. Those modified plans can offer amazing options for solidifying the practice of fasting, but they are not the model of fasting we find in Scripture and are not the fasting we see coupled with prayer. I do not fault people for using the word *fast* operatively, but I do take a firm stance on what fasting is so we do not fast amiss. Almost all the bodily benefits and beautiful regenerative processes of fasting happen when we abstain from food completely, and I believe our good God designed it that way for a purpose.

Our culture is awakening to the incredible benefits of fasting. A 2022 Real Research survey of fifty thousand people found that 80 percent of respondents were familiar with intermittent fasting and that of those, 75 percent had tried it at some point.[1] All you need to do is check Google or YouTube to see how popular intermittent fasting and other models are becoming. Fasting is cool now and sits alongside more well-known diets, like keto. Lent has also contributed to the renewed social awareness on fasting as various celebrities, such as Mark Wahlberg and Stephen Colbert, have been seen across social-media outlets with the telltale cross symbol to signify Ash Wednesday, the onset of the Lenten season.

Yet, for all the cultural acceptance, there remains little understanding in the Western church about the practice of fasting. It's time we reclaim this ancient wisdom.

FASTING AS SABBATH

The most important thing to know as we dive into fasting and its implications on the body is the spiritual principle around fasting: the Sabbath. When you fast, your body is literally in observance of the Sabbath. Though a lot happens at a biological level during a fast, the switching off of normal digestion gives the body much-needed rest.

Let's go a little deeper into the correlation between fasting and the Sabbath. From its first mention, God has always been serious about the Sabbath. Observing it was truly serious business. Take a look at these references:

- Genesis 2:2–3: "On the seventh day God ended His work which He had done, and He rested on the seventh day from all His work which He had done. Then God blessed the seventh day and sanctified it, because in it He rested from all His work which God had created and made."
- Exodus 20:8–10: "Remember the Sabbath day, to keep it holy. Six days you shall labor and do all your work, but the seventh day is the Sabbath of the LORD your God."
- Exodus 35:2: "Work shall be done for six days, but the seventh day shall be a holy day for you, a Sabbath of rest to the LORD. Whoever does any work on it shall be put to death."
- Leviticus 16:31: "It is a sabbath of solemn rest for you, and you shall afflict your souls. It is a statute forever."
- Isaiah 58:13–14: "If you turn away your foot from the Sabbath, from doing your pleasure on My holy day, and call the Sabbath a delight, the holy day of the LORD honorable, and shall honor Him, not doing your own ways, nor finding your own pleasure, nor speaking your own words, then you shall delight yourself in the LORD; and I will cause you to ride on the high hills of the earth."

The commands to obey the Sabbath are interwoven into God's narrative, timeline, and redemptive arc from Genesis to Revelation.

There are two themes across time and testament that we find consistent with the Sabbath: consecration and rest. Those are the two spiritual legs the Sabbath—and, consequently, fasting—stands upon.

CONSECRATION

The word *consecration* speaks to the whole ethos of fasting:

> *Consecrate* a fast,
>   call a solemn assembly;
> Gather the elders
>   and all the inhabitants of the land
> to the house of the LORD your God,
>   and cry out to the LORD.
>   (Joel 1:14, ESV)

The verse doesn't say to *start* a fast or *engage in* a fast; it says to *consecrate* a fast. When we fast, a restful, quiet, calm, solemn, and consecrated demeanor should be our disposition and heart posture. In fasting, we hold our hearts before God with silence and trembling, waiting for His fiery judgment to cauterize all that does not belong to or please Him. I've seen so many people initiate fasts but fill their days with movies, music, or entertainment to distract them from the discomfort of the process. That is a diet, not a fast. That is merely abstinence from suste- nance. Anytime we do what we want when we fast simply means we have missed the overall point and therefore have fasted amiss:

> "Why have we fasted," they say, "and You have not
>   seen?
> Why have we afflicted our souls, and You take no
>   notice?"
> In fact, in the day of your fast you find pleasure,
> And exploit all your laborers.
>   (Isaiah 58:3)

"In the day of your fast you find pleasure." What an indict- ment! Fasting is and should be an utter affliction of our souls before God, accompanied by a godly sorrow at the house of merchandise we have made our hearts—and His home. Absti- nence from food is not fasting; consecrating ourselves unto God by sacrificing food is:

> The LORD said to Moses, "Go to the people and consecrate them today and tomorrow, and let them wash their clothes. And let them be ready for the third day. For on the third day the LORD will come down upon Mount Sinai in the sight of all the people." (Exodus 19:10–11)

"Consecrate yourselves so you can hear when I come near." That was the mandate. Humbled souls, clean and yielded hearts, still and attentive minds to God and His will—those should be at the heart of fasting.

Consecration speaks to a state of being set apart, not just *from* something but *for* something. Preparation and purpose are central to the process. Every mention of the Sabbath tells us that we are to sanctify it as holy unto the Lord. It's *His* day! Our observance of it, though beneficial to us, should ultimately bring Him glory because God is most glorified by us when we are obedient to Him. That is why fasting is more than mere abstinence from food. God's command for hearts of consecration is why we are to refrain from seeking our pleasure in the Sabbath. And the New English Translation really brings it home:

> You must observe the Sabbath
> rather than doing anything you please on my holy day.
> You must look forward to the Sabbath
> and treat the LORD's holy day with respect.
> You must treat it with respect by refraining from your
>   normal activities,
> and by refraining from your selfish pursuits and from
>   making business deals.
> (Isaiah 58:13)

That passage really moves the idea of consecration into clear view. Our fasted lives should refrain from these things:

- normal activities
- selfish pursuits
- making business deals

I believe that the principle is what is being highlighted here and not necessarily the law. When the Bible speaks to abstaining from normal activities, I don't think it is banning us from such everyday activities as picking up kids from school or the things that need to be done for furthering life as we know it; it speaks to a consecrated disposition, a clear break from being controlled by those activities and chores. I believe a good, God-honoring fast is one in which we bring into submission and offer unto God as a pleasing sacrifice the following:

- normal activities—ourselves
- selfish pursuits—our senses
- making business deals—our sustenance

An offering of ourselves, our senses, and our substance. That is the true heart of worship, the ultimate posture of dependence upon the Lord. That is the epitome of subservience. Can you think of a worthier offering for us, as priests created to live and minister before the Lord (see 1 Peter 2:9), to bring before God, who honors obedience more than sacrifice?

Fasting is not a stand-alone practice but more like an approach protocol the children of Israel were given when going into the temple, according to the books of the biblical law. Fasting prepares us for worship, prayer, and drawing near to the presence of God. We bring ourselves before Him. We engage our senses in worshipping Him, and we offer our substance to honor Him, all as acts of worship, sacrifices pleasing to the Lord.

We feel the process of consecration acutely during the first few days of fasting. In those early days, I often refer to this simple prayer, which I've come to call the Prayer of Lordship, as my fasting examen of sorts, especially during the turbulent early days of the fast, when everything in and around me is telling me to quit:

> Father,
> You are Lord of myself and all my self loves.
> You own all my senses.
> You, Lord, are my sustenance.
> You alone satisfy.

I always slowly, deliberately, and reverently posture myself to pray, pausing between each statement to search God and allow Him to search me in turn. I will sometimes go through all the sensations that feel pressing, surrendering each one to Him as I pray. For example, I'll say, "Father, I thank You that my sight is consecrated unto You. I make a covenant with my eyes, as Job did,[2] to watch, read, and gaze upon only what pleases You." At another time, I may pray simply, "Father, I thank You that my appetites are consecrated unto You." Another beautiful prayer would be Philippians 4:8–9, which I use to focus, meditate, and whisper back to God reverent thoughts of all things noble, just, pure, lovely, virtuous, and praiseworthy.

That simple, contextualized examen has been a tremendous grounding practice for me because fasting is painful at times and a deeply introspective undertaking. When I carry a yielded heart in fasting, things the Holy Spirit is dealing with come to my attention and can be dealt with only by turning them over to the Refiner. When I feel hunger (or greed) come up, I humbly give Him lordship over it and thank Him that the Cross of Jesus and the sanctification of His Spirit covers me. Sometimes the habits, behaviors, and passions I thought were dead are dredged up by the fast so the Holy Spirit can deal with them.

The temptation of these hard days (and the natural response) is either fight or flight, but we should never wrestle our way toward an escape, because the entire disposition of a fasted soul is yieldedness. When we say yes to fasting, we say one giant yes to God and His sovereign cleansing work in our life and He always responds, lovingly showing up with a smile and a mop and bucket full of His cleaning supplies. One decisive yes in fasting is a definitive no to anything in our thoughts, attitudes, and appetites misaligned with Him, for the duration of our fast and hopefully our lives.

If I feel boredom during the day, I meditate on thoughts of His lordship over my pleasure and feast on those. We don't consecrate a fast and then wake up and throw ourselves to the will and whims of our scorned flesh. The fasted life is a conscious, curated one—a literal, living sacrifice.

Now, this is all well and good, you may think, *but some of us have jobs and commitments.* Great point. When I choose to fast, I typically do it on a day I have off from work or during a period when my calendar isn't as pressing. For example, I have always fasted on my birthday because I tend to have more control of my schedule that day. In biblical times, there would be a moratorium of all activities during fasts and Sabbaths, so the principle of structuring our fasts around days without work is not such a maverick concept. We cannot give God what costs us nothing.

Realistically, we can still fast and go about the affairs of our day as long as our hearts are consecrated unto Him. Remember, consecration, and not necessarily cessation of all work, is primarily what the Lord desires and consequently blesses. The renowned French monk and mystic known as Brother Lawrence embodies this in *The Practice of the Presence of God*.[3] In that little book, he tells how he would commune with God constantly, even while washing dishes, and people would come for miles to be within proximity of his devotion. The degree may vary based on schedule and commitment, but I believe we find time for the things we truly value. Before fitting fasting into the crevices of our already packed days, we should, to the best of our ability, make a concerted effort to set aside days we can spend fasting and devoting prayer to God.

Enduring the Process of Fasted Consecration

Fasting should always begin with our recklessly abandoning ourselves to the mercy of God and His sustaining grace. Even though the pain and discomfort are primarily felt in our bodies, it is still a deeply spiritual work and can be sustained only by the grace of God. Throughout my various fasts, I have found that without an anchor for my soul, I always struggle and have broken my fast in frustration at its futility, some secret shame, or moments of weakness that felt as though they would last forever.

That is why Scripture, worship, and remembering the truths of God's nature and His promises are so important for buoying our souls, brains, emotions, and wills. Contrary to popular coaching and belief, willpower will not sustain us through a water fast, but anchoring ourselves in *Him* will. Ninety-nine percent of the warfare in fasting will happen in the mind. The body weaponizes the mind to convince us to eat because its primary function is to keep us alive. (More on that as we dive deeper into the physiology of fasting.) Without something to anchor our souls and latch our hope to, we will succumb to discouragement and quit.

I love what Hebrews 6:19 says: "This hope we have as an anchor of the soul, both sure and steadfast, and which enters the Presence behind the veil." When our souls (again, which includes our minds, wills, and emotions) go haywire, we can quiet them by anchoring them to the hope of the most beautiful of outcomes. This hope in God, His path and purpose for us all, becomes central to our fasted offering. We can find reminders of this hope, and the grand narrative of God's kingdom story, in a favorite worship song or hymn, a book, or a passage of Scripture—anything that helps us rest in Him as we fast.

I have found Brother Lawrence's book to be deeply grounding. It is a phenomenal read and most worthwhile investment. One of my favorite quotes goes like this:

That we should establish ourselves in a sense of God's Presence, by continually conversing with Him. That it was a shameful thing to quit His conversation, to think of trifles and fooleries.

That we should feed and nourish our souls with high notions of God, which would yield us great joy in being devoted to Him.[4]

REST

The second pillar on the foundation of the Sabbath is rest. Fasting guides the entire body into a state of active rest so it can begin the work of healing and rejuvenation. This principle is interwoven everywhere throughout the Bible.

Psalm 127:2 reminds us of the futility of striving without God-given rest. The most famous of passages, Psalm 23, assures us that God shepherds us along still waters, symbolizing inner peace and rest (verse 2). Psalm 62:1–2 speaks to a restful posture of silence in solitude as we wait for the Lord's deliverance, finding rest and silence in God alone. In Joshua 23:1, we discover that God granted Israel rest after conquering the Promised Land.

Rest is used metaphorically all throughout Scripture. Zion, God's "dwelling place" (Psalm 132:13), is called His resting place. Even the most celebrated time of social reform in Jewish antiquity, the year of Jubilee (see Leviticus 25:8–55), was a time of rest for those in slavery and for the very land itself.

This quote from Rabbi Abraham Joshua Heschel in his book *The Sabbath* ties it all together:

Six days a week we seek to dominate the world, on the seventh day we try to dominate the self.[5]

In the tempestuous ocean of time and toil there are islands of stillness where man may enter a harbor and reclaim his dignity. The island is the seventh day, the Sabbath, a day of detachment from things, instruments and practical affairs as well as of attachment to the spirit.[6]

Rest is far beyond being just a period of inactivity; it's a deep, gestational state in which all life, growth, and connection begin and thrive:

> Thus says the Lord GOD, the Holy One of Israel:
> "In returning and rest you shall be saved;
> In quietness and confidence shall be your strength."
> But you would not.
> (Isaiah 30:15)

In God's upside-down, antithetical kingdom, we are created from a place of rest in the garden of rest, commanded to rest, and, through the finished work of Jesus, enter into, live, move, and have our being in the rest that is Jesus.

The book of Hebrews could be branded as a symposium on rest:

> There remains therefore a rest for the people of God. For he who has entered His rest has himself also ceased from his works as God did from His.
>
> Let us therefore be diligent to enter that rest, lest anyone fall according to the same example of disobedience. (4:9–11)

Rest is the position that leads to quietness. Let me clarify that. Rest is the position; quietness is the disposition. In a spiritually fasted state, we are in rest, and the tangible expression through us is one of quietness. Generally, when you begin a fast, you enter a time of an uncomfortable shift as your body moves from its normal habits into a fasting state. But after that initial shift, you wake up one day and your entire being is at rest.

The command of the Sabbath is rest, the culture of consecration is rest, the pinnacle of the fasted state is rest, and the call to a fasted lifestyle is a call to rest.

5

The Posture

Ask me and I will tell you remarkable secrets
you do not know about things to come.
—Jeremiah 33:3, NLT

MOST PEOPLE ASSUME THAT communication is the highest use of language, but I would like to propose that communion, not communication, is the highest use of language.

In the natural evolution of language, comprehension is initially prioritized over connection. People communicate to get a point across so the recipient of said communication can do something and move the overall initiative forward. As language becomes more established, communication becomes a tool that people use to connect in more intimate ways. That becomes the birth of art, poetry, and artistic expressions of language. I'm reminded of this brilliant and convicting quote found in a letter from the second American president, John Adams, to his wife, Abigail:

I must study Politicks and War that my sons may have liberty to study Mathematicks and Philosophy. . . . Geography, natural History, Naval Architecture, navigation, Commerce and Agriculture, in order to give their Children a right to study Painting, Poetry, Musick, Architecture, Statuary, Tapestry and Porcelaine.[1]

I am a sucker for the linguistic brilliance of the Founding Fathers, and I believe Adams's correspondence captures the unavoidable shift in generational priorities as language and culture mature.

Following a similar pattern, prayer may start out as a tool to submit requests, but as we grow in our walks with Christ, it becomes the modality for communion and connection.

There are incredible fringe benefits to prayer, and our good Father delights to give us all good things when we ask. "Do not fear, little flock, for it is your Father's good pleasure to give you the kingdom," Luke 12:32 tells us, and Romans 8:32 adds, "He who did not spare His own Son, but delivered Him up for us all, how shall He not with Him also freely give us all things?" Receiving, however, is not the primary purpose of prayer.

In any new relationship, our conversation is at first superficial. We ask generic questions, and our connections are usually centered around a shared value, goal, or ideal. But the deeper the relationship grows, the more we learn to love the other person and the more we become sensitive to the notion of being used by them. God creates us for communion, but like every child, we first relate to Him based on our wants and needs until, in maturity, we learn to love, appreciate, and prefer His very essence and presence.

In its infancy, prayer is a modality for utility; in its maturity, prayer is a landscape for learning love. In the place of prayer, we commune with our beloved in the cool of the day like Adam and Eve did. We learn His heart, we learn His ways, and we consequently create everything around us in His image, because the by-product of intimacy will always be creation.

MADE TO CALL ON GOD

The journey to spiritual maturity begins when the disciplines of the way become the rule of life we live by. That is where we pray with fervency because we are praying *for* something tangible. As God answers our prayers, our trust and reliance on Him grows and we develop a personal history with Him in the process. That history becomes the foundation for our convictions and flourishes into an unshakable faith like the heroes of Hebrews 11 are known for.

I come from an unapologetically praying household where prayer transcended its mere spiritual utility and was ingrained in us as a staunch family value. Living in a spiritually aware culture meant we regularly relied on God's divine protection during spiritual warfare. Being a family of subsistence farmers in a nation known for unpredictable rainfall as well as devastating droughts meant we had to constantly pray for miraculous sustenance. But as you can imagine, prayers of desperation and survival are rarely prayers of communion that bring us closer to God and foster a lifestyle of abiding. No, these are a different breed of prayers. These are outer-court petitions with specific urgency and grit. These are prayers that wrestle with God as Jacob did and scream, "I will not let You go unless You bless me!" (Genesis 32:26).

We see prayers of desperation over and over in the Gospels. Bereaved mothers, grieving fathers, desperate outcasts, the lame, and the lepers are all too familiar with these prayers. They are the prayers that place a demand on God's mighty hand and His miraculous arm of old. I had to pray this kind of very painful prayer not too long ago.

My older sister, Nomusa (her name means "Mother of Mercy"), who is based in the United Kingdom, had been ill for a while and was diagnosed with end-stage kidney failure. I remember getting the call from my brother Thando (his full name, Thandolwenkosi, means "Love of God"). He said, "On top of the renal failure, Nomusa has just contracted Covid. The doctors say she is in isolation on a ventilator and this is the end of the end. If I were you, I'd book my travel and say your goodbyes, as she may not be coherent or responsive in another day or two."

And right then, my world began spinning. By God's grace, we had not buried a single sibling from the thirteen of us, and the only loss had been the loss of our father, in the natural and blessed order of things. Ubuntu philosophy states that the biggest blessing a father can have is to never bury a son but to precede them and pave their way into the afterlife. I remember asking my wife, Pam, if she wanted to join me on what would be a journey far different from our vacation getaways. She agreed, and we somberly prepared ourselves for it.

As I packed, I noticed Pete Greig's book *Dirty Glory*[2] on my bedside table. I had met Pete and his amazing wife, Sammy, for the first time a few weeks before when we spoke at the same conference, and I was deeply marked by his calm confidence in the power of God and prayer. His book *Red Moon Rising*[3] was required reading at the seminary I went to, and I was well aware of this giant in the faith whom God had entrusted with a nonstop global prayer movement (24-7 Prayer)[4] that now reaches approximately seventy-eight countries. At the conference, we took time to eat lunch together, during which I asked question upon question about prayer, fasting, and revival and they courteously indulged me in incredible conversation. At the end of the lunch, I asked Pete and Sammy to pray over me, to which they happily agreed, and they prayed a sincere prayer that I would hunger more deeply for prayer. They also graciously gave me copies of their books and scribbled encouraging words on the inner flaps. The book on the nightstand was the book I now tossed into my travel bag.

And it changed everything.

I had a ten-hour flight from Dallas to London, and I couldn't rest or engage in entertainment, as my body had somehow begun its natural grieving process. It is a funny business grieving the living-yet-leaving. I wanted to squeeze meaning out of every present moment while reminiscing on the happy past as well as looking ahead to the bereft future without this person in it. My mind was in a state of shock, and my internal processing felt shaky. So to steady my nerves and avoid being the ugly-crying Black dude on the flight, I started to read Pete's book, and something in me came alive.

See, something had fundamentally shifted in me since I

came to the United States. Due to the abundance of provision and prosperity found in America, very few situations warranted strong prayers of intervention. I didn't have to flex my muscle for desperation prayer quite as often, and it had seriously atrophied. I had lulled myself into accepting a laissez-faire attitude toward prayer. I had told myself that God is sovereign and He will where He wills and will not where He does not. I had embraced a theology of powerlessness and blamed it on sovereignty, and that theology remained untested until desperation shattered my faulty mold.

I read Pete's book with a respectful skepticism at first that slowly morphed into incredulity before settling into awe. In one of the chapters, Pete makes a compelling case for how we can approach God and plead for the miraculous on behalf of our loved ones. He tells the horror story of how his and Sammy's young son had taken what should have been a lethal dose of prescription medicines and they had rallied an army and prayed while watching the Lord work a miracle to save the child's life. Reading that was like an adrenaline shot to my soul! It felt like the awakening moment in a movie when the superhero discovers their powers or when an eagle stretches its full wingspan and dives off the cliff for the first time. My prayer-warrior heritage roared within me and I was reborn. And in that sacred moment of rebirth, I remembered something:

Humankind was made to call on God.

From the early days of Adam and Eve engaging with their creator, through our personal experiences, until the glimpse into eternity future we see in the book of Revelation, we were meant to dialogue with God.

That same book of the Bible tells us that God, at the foundation of the world, slew the lamb (see 13:8), which was the propitiation that would bridge the communication gap between God and mankind that occurred when Adam and Eve sinned. Before God made us, He set in motion two things: a sacrifice to redeem us to Himself, and an altar so we could contact Him. (Think of E.T. and his phone.) In the Old Testament, every notable encounter with God (or gods) happened around an altar, and after the death of Christ, that altar shifted and became our hearts. And by the blood of Jesus sprinkled on it, we can call on God anytime.

If we zoom out far enough and examine the entire Bible from Genesis to Revelation, we notice a pattern. We notice that regardless of time and space, heaven has always responded to man's cries.

Genesis 4:26 says, "As for Seth, to him also a son was born; and he named him Enosh. Then men began to call on the name of the Lord." As I read that genealogy, I noticed something very interesting: When the Lord wanted to set the earth back on the track of its created mandate, He began with Enosh, as he was the first redemptive offshoot after the debacle between Adam and Eve's two sons Cain and Abel. And God responded. And since that moment and across time and history, God has *always* responded to the call of man.

An interesting tidbit I found meaningful and personally powerful is that the name *Enosh* in Hebrew means human, or mortal man.[5] That time of Enosh, the mortal man, marked the beginning of epochs when mortal men could (and frequently did) call on the name of the Lord and the Lord would respond. The Hebrew word for *Lord* in that particular scripture is the tetragrammaton YHWH. *Tetragrammaton* means "four letters" in Greek and represents the most sacred name for God in Judaism. This is interesting to note because that name was what the Hebrew people referred to as God's covenant name, and it reveals a particular aspect of God's nature: that He acts in history, establishes a covenant relationship with His people, and fulfills His promises. If I paraphrased that verse with all the power of the Hebrew context nuanced into our English language, it might go something like this: "In the days of the mortal man (Enosh), men began to call on the name of the God of covenant, who swore His provision, protection, and presence to His people for all time (YHWH)." Isn't that powerful?

When we call on this God of covenant, we can expect Him to respond exceedingly and abundantly above the scope of our petitions because along with being an all-hearing God, YHWH is also all-powerful. Out of respect of not just His name but also His office, observant Jews traditionally avoid directly pronouncing YHWH. They say *Adonai,* meaning "Lord," or *Hashem,* meaning "the name." In the Jewish culture, similar to Ubuntu, names are more than simply identity markers but primarily denote reputation and role. Names speak to what you do and your ability to do—that is, your authority—because names are synonymous with office, much like the English use of titles like *president.* The covenant name of *YHWH* tells us everything we need to know about the God who responds to our prayers.

This was a God who communicated with His creation, and this was a God who invited His people to cry out to Him, because this is a God who promises to answer. We see that anchored in Jeremiah 33:3: "Call to me and I will answer you and tell you great and unsearchable things you do not know" (NIV).

I love the rich nuance in all the rhetoric—the descriptors for the types of things that shall be revealed to us for the simple price of an ask. "Unsearchable things," the New International Version tells us. The New Living Translation renders them "remarkable secrets." The Christian Standard Bible calls them "incomprehensible." All ours, and all a distressed, heartfelt, importunate cry away.

That realization hit me like a ton of bricks and hooked me like the lifeline it is. I could cry out in prayer on behalf of my sister, and this all-powerful covenant God had the care to hear and the capacity to respond. And what's more, my cry was not a bother to Him; rather, it was my birthright! We are meant to call and cry out to God. Every other page in Scripture is a narrative of humanity crying out to God and Him responding. In the first chapter of 1 Samuel, we meet Hannah, a woman in deep anguish from barrenness. She taps into her birthright, calls upon the Lord, and from that deep place of anguish prays for a child. God hears her plea and blesses her with Samuel.

If there were such a thing as a calling-on-God master class, Daniel would be the professor. His entire story is one big ask of God after another, from dream interpretation to defying the king's decree, which lands him in the lions' den.

During a showdown with false prophets in 1 Kings 18, Elijah prays boldly and God consumes his sacrifice with fire from heaven, demonstrating His almighty power.

In 2 Kings 20, King Hezekiah, facing death, fervently prays to God. God extends his life by fifteen years.

After disobeying God, our favorite recalcitrant, Jonah, repents inside the belly of a giant fish (see Jonah 2). God hears his prayer and delivers him.

This call-and-response promise doesn't exist only in the Old Testament. Jesus frequently withdraws to pray, such as before choosing His disciples (see Luke 6:12–13) or in the Garden of Gethsemane (see Matthew 26:36–45). God strengthens and guides Him.

In Acts 12:1–10, Peter is imprisoned by the tyrannical tetrarch of the day, King Herod. The church fervently prays for his release, and in miraculous response, an angel of the Lord stages the second-most daring prison break in canonized history.

I say *second* because the first is done by Paul and Silas in Acts 16:16–40. After being brutally beaten and imprisoned, they begin praying and singing hymns from the belly of the prison, and YHWH responds with an earthquake that unlocks their chains and leads to the jailer's conversion.

In Acts 10, we see how a Gentile centurion named Cornelius and his family seek God earnestly. God directs both Cornelius and Peter, setting in motion the spread of the gospel beyond the Jewish community. The promise of a hearing, responsive God is for all humanity. Regardless of our color or caste, the ability to call upon the Lord is our birthright.

With that revelation and reminder, my heart came alive and I paid the exorbitant price to access intercontinental Wi-Fi and got to work. I found the latest picture of my sister in the hospital, posted it on social media, and asked for prayer support from the masses. I remembered this promise in Matthew 18:19: "If two of you agree on earth concerning anything that they ask, it will be done for them by My Father in heaven."

I began texting every prayer warrior I knew—the scrappy African, Middle Eastern, Asian, Hispanic, and been-through-the-fire White ones. I wanted everyone whose experience with prayer had been forged and finessed through adversity warring on my side. I sent the picture and my request to prayer groups, and I reached out to all the praying grandmas who had ever called me "son." I wasn't merely sharing a prayer request; I was building an army.

I would like to take this time to highlight a crucial piece of strategy in prayer, and that is the power of precedent. Most people in the world whose predominant governmental system is democracy understand the power and infallibility of a country's constitution, and for us kingdom denizens, God's Word is our constitution. If you see that God did something in Scripture, that's the precedent for you to boldly approach Him and say, "Lord, please do for me what You did for them."

That's why testimony is so powerful. Remembering and telling what God has done builds faith. And what happens when faith is built? Unbelief wanes and our spirits can clearly communicate with heaven so His Spirit can do its work. It's not humility to hide what the Lord has done in our lives. We have a responsibility to shout it from the rooftops! Someone's battle is dependent on our precedent! God's acts are irreversible and His promises irrevocable. As my Pentecostal friends used to say, "If He said it, then that settles it!"

As soon as I'd sent and sounded the alarm for urgent prayer, I began to pray. Now, if there was ever a theological case study for praying in the spirit, I was the walking, talking, desperate embodiment of it! In Romans 8, Paul states,

> The Spirit also helps in our weaknesses. For we do not know what we should pray for as we ought, but the Spirit Himself makes intercession for us with groanings which cannot be uttered. Now He who searches the hearts knows what the mind of the Spirit is, because He makes intercession for the saints according to the will of God. (verses 26–27)

I was the epitome of weakness. I did not know how to pray as I ought. My soul was screaming worst-case scenarios and drowning my spirit. I had no medical know-how and was too unsettled to pray from a space of faith and conviction, so all I could do was allow God's Holy Spirit, my divine intercessor, to pray through me. I started pacing up and down during that flight, and I didn't care who saw my charismatic showing—I was desperate! I didn't want to bury my sister, and the longer I thought of God's promises and meditated on His nature, the more convinced I became of His will and His zeal to heal her.

To cut a long and beautiful story short, miraculous things happened when we landed. The Holy Spirit told us when to head to the hospital, and when we got there, my sister was being wheeled to a room for a procedure. We got to see and pray healing over her and share stories of all the people praying for her. We would not have been allowed to see her had we gotten there at any other time. That very day, she began what her doctor called an impossible miracle, and she is still alive and with us!

God still does miracles, and the experiences and testimonies speak for themselves. We were made to communicate with God. He loves it when we call on Him when we are facing a bleak diagnosis, an impossibility with a deadline coming up, or any kind of desperate situation. And He loves it when we call on Him to seek His presence, learn His ways, and commune with His Spirit.

FASTING PREPARES AND CALMS

We were made to communicate with God, but prayer is more than sending up our request lists. And fasting is more than attempting to gain God's attention. As we seek to grow in our prayer practice, there are simple yet potent steps we can learn to aid us toward maturity.

Approaching royalty requires a significant level of detail, decorum, and honor. How much more important is protocol when approaching *divine* royalty? Fasting prepares us for a divine encounter, and alongside prayer, it creates an intersubjective space for communing with royalty. So it behooves us to learn the protocol of approach.

Esther was well acquainted with the dangers of flippantly

approaching royalty, and when she knew she would have to make an unsummoned appearance, she spent considerable time preparing herself. She *fasted* and had the support of an entire praying nation as she approached King Ahasuerus at her own peril. Because of her careful preparation, her story became a mighty testament to the glory of a God who loves to intervene in the affairs of His people.

Fasting conditions us, clothes us rightly, and recalibrates our dispositions as we approach God to petition Him for the impossible. Fasting quiets the soul so we can gain clarity. Anyone who has fasted for extended periods of time knows the deep, soulful quietness that forms from within. I struggle to find the right words because, much like with petrichor, the unmistakable fragrance that lingers after a good rain, it is hard to describe if you haven't experienced it. The best I can come up with is the word *quietness*. While silence is the absence of sound, quietness can be described as the presence of stillness. Unlike with silence, quietness doesn't feel empty.

A similar idea is the Japanese concept of *ma*. Ma speaks to the empty space in between things and is the informing philosophy behind the minimalist aesthetic we see in Japanese homes. Ma represents the essence of space and time, integral aspects of Japanese aesthetics and philosophy, embodying the pause between actions, the silence within music, and the empty space in visual art. It's not merely a gap; it's a space filled with potential where the unspoken and the explicit coexist in harmony, inviting contemplation and understanding. In ma, the absence is as meaningful as the presence, encouraging mindfulness and appreciation of the moment. This concept teaches us the value of the intangible, emphasizing that what is not there can shape and define our experience as much as what *is* there. Through ma, we learn to perceive the world beyond the physical, recognizing the beauty and significance in the spaces between. That, I believe, comes closest to describing the tangible peace we feel when we are fasting. We feel it, we embody it, and we become proxies of said peace.

I can always tell when I'm around a person who has adopted a lifestyle of fasting, because not only are they calm but they exist as a calming presence and leave a deep imprint of peace in every social dynamic. That calmness flows from a heart rightly enthroned. When the Prince of Peace inhabits the throne of your heart, you become a carrier and a creature of peace.

FASTING CLEANSES

In John 2:13–15, we encounter Jesus doing something somewhat shocking:

> The Passover of the Jews was at hand, and Jesus went up to Jerusalem. And He found in the temple those who sold oxen and sheep and doves, and the money changers doing business. When He had made a whip of cords, He drove them all out of the temple, with the sheep and the oxen, and poured out the changers' money and overturned the tables.

Peace-loving Jesus literally makes a whip! That speaks to a highly premeditated act. Jesus then takes this instrument of corrective chaos and uses it to kick everyone out of the temple! Now, whether you've seen it on TV or in person, a Middle Eastern market setting is a bustling, busy place filled with a hodgepodge of people earning their livelihood. There is a natural aggression required to be competitive in an open market. I remember every Christmastime in Bulawayo, my African hometown, we would slaughter a goat to feed everyone who would visit for the festive season, and we would often have to go into the market for the daunting task of purchasing said goat.

My father would always take along four or five of us boys as a show of strength so we would not be intimidated into accepting inferior stock at an inflated price. We would show up, walk condescendingly through the flock, and pick the one we wanted. The livestock dealers were always stocky, sun seared, and rough, and I was always intimidated by their bottom-line attitudes.

Well, in a surprising behavioral shift, Jesus descends on their entire operation whip akimbo:

He said to them, . . . " 'My house shall be called a house of prayer,' but you have made it a 'den of thieves.' "
Then the blind and the lame came to Him in the temple, and He healed them. (Matthew 21:13–14)

That statement, at face value, may seem a bit harsh and somewhat ruthless, but Jesus's ruthlessness was justified because two things more nefarious and corrupt than mere livestock commodity were taking place.

It is important to note that the sellers and money changers had set up shop in the court of Gentiles,[6] the one place in the temple where non-Jewish people could go to worship God, as they were forbidden from entering the inner courts. This was a gross affront on God's will and design of His temple as the house of prayer for "all nations." Similarly, when we allow ordinary things to crowd our sacred hearts, they will always take space from those things that truly matter to God.

In a religious context that relied on daily, weekly, and annual sacrifices, this unending cycle of avarice brought considerable wealth to all the parties involved, especially the priests.[7] In Exodus 22:25, God stated to Israel, "If you lend money to any of My people who are poor among you, you shall not be like a moneylender to him; you shall not charge him interest." And Leviticus 25:35–37 reads,

> If one of your brethren becomes poor, and falls into poverty among you, then you shall help him, like a stranger or a sojourner, that he may live with you. Take no usury or interest from him; but fear your God, that your brother may live with you. You shall not lend him your money for usury, nor lend him your food at a profit.

God's will about justice and inflated lending practices had been made clear to all Israel, so everyone, especially the priests, were aware of their own roles and complicity in these infractions. Those were the same priests who were supposed to represent the heart of God but had settled for making money and, by doing so, committed a grave sin. Is it any wonder that the greed of the priests that had turned a space of intimacy and petition into a common market incurred the wrath and whip of the Son of God?

The moral of Jesus cleansing the temple is apparent, but I think the most important lesson for us is in its symbolism. Jesus cleansed His temple, and now, post-Resurrection, the temple of God is in us, body, soul, and spirit: "Do you not know that your body is the temple of the Holy Spirit who is in you, whom you have from God, and you are not your own?" (1 Corinthians 6:19).

When left unchecked or untended, our heart temples can quickly become places of commerce, much like my African marketplace. In this distracted economy, our internal marketplaces for ideas need to be constantly and ruthlessly cleansed and all their altars consecrated.

Due to life, greed, and the epidemic of distraction (I recommend John Mark Comer's book *The Ruthless Elimination of Hurry* for both the diagnosis and prognosis of this), our temples become overcrowded with various noises and voices. And much like the situation in the temple, what should have been a sanctuary for God and solitude becomes commoditized and sullied.

Once Jesus sent all the sellers outside, the blind and the lame then came and He healed them. Healing began after the temple was cleansed.

That is what I believe fasting does for us. It acts as an abrasive, calibrating tool for our souls and cleanses our temples. Then and only then can the true healing begin. It's interesting to note that Jesus did that temple cleansing twice: once at the beginning and then again at the end of His life and ministry.[8] Consecration must be a deliberate and ongoing practice, built into the personal culture and cadence of our walks.

Proverbs 4:23 cautions us to guard our hearts with all diligence, for out of them flow our lives. Our hearts are like streams and gardens, which need tending to prevent algae or weeds from growing. When the sacred places in our hearts are left untended, undesirable habits and modes of operating begin. But fasting offers a beautiful practice and an incredible ally for not only getting our hearts back to optimum state but also keeping them holy, clean, and open to the divine flow.

6

Fasting and Our Physiology

OUR PHYSIOLOGY IS SACRED. That is the first truth we need to master in the basics of fasting. The body's physiology is coded and conditioned by God to prioritize two things: preservation and propagation. Everything else—every physical activity, every hormone, every system—comes after those two primary functions. At the biological level, our bodies strive to stay alive long enough to procreate and raise the offspring until they can, in turn, procreate. As a result, our bodies reward our minds for choosing activities (like eating) that support their goals.

Our bodies achieve the prioritization of preservation and propagation by using hormones and neurotransmitters such as insulin and dopamine. Dopamine is often called the feel-good hormone. It acts as a messenger between brain cells. When you experience something rewarding (like eating your favorite food), your brain releases dopamine. That release teaches your brain to want to repeat the action. That is because the body primarily works on a reward and punishment system: pain and pleasure.[1]

Not only is dopamine released in general, but it is released in strategic ways as well. Our bodies prioritize caloric intake, not necessarily quality nutrition. That is why foods that contain salt, oil, or sugar (or what is called the SOS diet), such as pizza and doughnuts, are more pleasurable than, say, a celery stick or salad. We can fine-tune our palates to crave leaner and cleaner cuisine by forcing ourselves to enjoy it and, by so doing, hack our dopamine production, but at a base level, we are drawn to the foods with high carbohydrates because high-carb foods like bread and pasta contain glucose, locked up in long, complex chains called starches. When our bodies break down the glucose, that form of sugar gives us energy and triggers a reward response in our brains, making us feel good. Dr. Pradip Jamnadas, known for his work on the health benefits of water fasting, says the body was designed that way for the Paleolithic man, who had to hunt and gather food. Because of Paleolithic man's intermittent-fasting lifestyle and all-natural diet, his metabolism always had time to break down food and store energy.[2] His whole system was in a constant state of equilibrium.

Our innovations became our dietary downfall, though, because the invention of the steel mill meant we could produce bread and other food at a rate faster than we could burn it, and so obesity and all our dietary problems set in. The supply overruns the demand, and with a twenty-four-hour consumption cycle, our bodies can no longer triage the intake, because now most of our food is overprocessed. Our bodies have no frame of reference on what to do in the allocation and breakdown of artificial food, so they use ridiculous amounts of energy to digest it. Eating processed food with complex compound structures that we can barely digest means that food is sitting in our guts longer and our bodies don't get any rest between meals. When food stays in our guts too long, it causes all sorts of bacteria to fester and grow, leading to complexities such as leaky gut and cancer.[3]

The hormone insulin, produced by the pancreas, turns all the food you eat into glucose for immediate energy, and fat for long-term storage.[4] Think of it as a key that opens the doors to your body's cells to let sugar (glucose) in from the blood for energy. The excess is stored as fat for use on a rainy day. As long as you ingest food on a regular basis, insulin regulates how much is utilized and how much is stored.

When you fast, however, your body doesn't get sugar from food, so your insulin level decreases. When it lowers past a certain threshold, it triggers a signal to your body to start burning the fat stores, rather than sugar, for energy. Imagine that your body is a busy kitchen and that insulin and dopamine are two of the staff members. Here's what they do and how they change jobs during a water fast.

Insulin

Job Title: Sugar-Storage Manager

Usual Duties: When you eat, insulin rushes in to grab all the sugar (glucose) from your food and stores it away in your muscles, liver, and fat cells. It's like putting extra grocery supplies into the pantry.

Fasting Shift: During a fast, no new food is arriving, so insulin starts taking a break. Because there's less sugar to manage, insulin levels drop. That is a signal for your body to start using the stored sugar in the pantry for energy.

Dopamine

Job Title: Good-Vibes Director

Usual Duties: Dopamine gives you a little burst of happiness when you do something good for yourself, like eating tasty food or achieving a goal. It's like getting an employee-of-the-month award!

Fasting Shift: During a longer fast, dopamine steps up its game. Its levels might rise, helping reduce hunger pangs and keeping you feeling a bit more motivated and focused. Think of it as the kitchen staff cheering one another on when there's extra work to do.

Now that we understand the basic overarching processes that occur when we fast, I'd like to walk us through what happens to our bodies from day one to day ten of a water fast. The reason I stop at day ten is that although our mileage, based on our dietary intake, may vary during fasting, most new processes have already kicked into gear by day ten, and they just go deeper with every passing day thereafter. The changes we'll experience in the first ten days are simply the beginning. There will still be many toxins that mitigate the potency of the bodily functions, but typically at ten days in, there is no external interference, and true growth and regeneration continues until the body processes are maximized.

This beneficial process period goes on until day forty, when the body kicks from a fasted state into starvation. Fasting more than forty days is dangerous to the body's health and not recommended at all.

FASTING DAY BY DAY

It may be helpful to visualize the first few days of a fast as an airplane flying through a storm. At first, you'll experience considerable turbulence, but if you continue, you'll break through the clouds and into the most beautiful, tranquil atmosphere. Such is the case with fasting. If you hold to your fast beyond the initial turbulence and let your body wean off your numerous addictions, self-regulate, clean up, and chemically balance, you will ultimately break into a state of rest, and the benefits are, literally, out of this world.

Day One: Burning Through Leftovers

During the first day of your water fast, your body will primarily rely on glycogen, a stored form of carbohydrates, for energy. This glycogen is found in your liver and muscles and is easily accessible for your body to use. Your insulin levels, which are responsible for regulating blood sugar, will start to decrease. At the same time, glucagon, a hormone that helps break down glycogen and fat, will increase. This shift in hormones is necessary to maintain your body's energy levels in the absence of food. You may feel the initial disorientation, which includes hunger pangs, especially around your usual mealtimes. That is simply because of conditioning. You may also experience mild fatigue or irritability as your body adjusts to using stored energy instead of readily available glucose.

Body Processes

Glycogenolysis: Your liver breaks down stored glycogen into glucose to maintain energy levels throughout the day.

Gluconeogenesis: As glycogen stores deplete, your liver starts producing glucose from non-carbohydrate sources (e.g., proteins and fats).

Insulin secretion: Pancreatic insulin release helps regulate blood-glucose levels by directing glucose into cells for energy.[5]

Day Two: Entering Ketosis

On the second day of your water fast, your body continues to adapt to the lack of external food sources. As your glycogen stores begin to deplete, your liver starts to convert fat into ketone bodies, which will serve as alternative fuel sources for your brain and body. This process, known as ketosis, occurs when your body doesn't have enough carbohydrates to burn for energy. As your body enters ketosis, you may experience symptoms such as bad breath, fatigue, and increased thirst. These symptoms are normal and typically subside as your body adjusts to the new metabolic state. Your hunger pangs may intensify initially as your body signals the need for more energy. This is usually where people panic because they are experiencing flu-like symptoms. This phenomenon is called "keto flu," with symptoms such as headaches, fatigue, nausea, and brain fog as your body adapts to a new fuel source. Hang in there!

Body Processes

Decreased insulin production: With less available glucose, your pancreas reduces insulin output.

Increased glucagon secretion: This hormone signals the liver to increase glycogen breakdown and glucose production.

Ketogenesis: The liver ramps up the conversion of fats into ketones as alternative fuel sources for the body.

Fat mobilization: Stored fats are released from adipose tissue (animal fat) to be broken down into fatty acids for ketone production.[6]

Day Three: Clear Thinking

By the third day of your water fast, your body has fully transitioned into ketosis. Your brain, which typically relies on glucose for energy, begins to adapt to using ketones as its primary fuel source. This adaptation can lead to improved mental clarity and focus. As your body becomes more efficient at burning fat for energy, you may notice a decrease in hunger and cravings. This is because ketones have an appetite-suppressing effect, which makes it easier to stick to your fast. The number one fear that people have about fasting usually has to do with hunger. They know what it's like to experience that initial hangry state when they have not eaten for a few hours, and they assume this will compound as the fast continues. Day three is usually the last time you feel hunger as ketones kick into gear. Another positive side effect you experience is improved mental clarity and focus due to the efficiency of ketones as an energy source for the brain. Think of it this way: Your fuel determines the cleanness of your burn. Wood, for example, will burn with leaner and cleaner smoke than, say, oil. It's the same with the brain. Much of the mental fog we experience is a result of the food we are eating. Day three typically brings with it a sense of increased energy stability without the highs and lows associated with blood-sugar fluctuations.

Day Four: Adapting to the New Normal

On the fourth day, your body becomes more efficient at utilizing ketones for energy, and the unpleasant keto-flu symptoms generally subside. Your levels of human growth hormone (HGH) start to increase. HGH plays a crucial role in maintaining lean muscle mass and promoting fat loss. The increased levels of HGH help preserve your muscle tissue and prevent muscle breakdown during the fast. This is important because maintaining your lean muscle mass is essential for keeping your metabolism running efficiently.

Body Processes

Hormone regulation: Ghrelin (hunger hormone) levels often decrease, while levels of satiety-promoting hormones, like leptin, adjust to a fasted state.

Improved insulin sensitivity: Even though insulin production is lowered, cells become more responsive to its effects, improving glucose regulation when food is reintroduced.[7]

Day Five: Cellular Spring-Cleaning

By the fifth day of your water fast, a process called autophagy begins to ramp up. Autophagy (from the Greek, a compound of *autos* [self] and *phagein* [eating]) is a natural cellular cleansing that breaks down and recycles old, damaged proteins and cellular components. During autophagy, your body "cleans house," removing dysfunctional cells and cellular debris. This process is thought to have anti-aging benefits and may help to reduce inflammation in the body. The way I like to explain it is if your heater wasn't working in your house, you would break up all the nonessential furniture to burn for warmth. Because autophagy is internal, occurring at a cellular level, you don't necessarily "feel" autophagy, even though the overall benefits are tangible and measurable in the health of the faster.

Body Processes

Autophagy: This cellular-recycling process significantly increases, removing damaged cellular components and promoting regeneration.

Reduced inflammation: Fasting can decrease systemic inflammation levels, contributing to overall health and wellness.

Improved mitochondrial function: Mitochondria become more efficient at producing energy.

Day Six: Finding a New Rhythm

At this point, you may notice improvements in your mental clarity and focus. This is because your brain has fully adapted to using ketone bodies for fuel, which can provide steady and efficient energy sources. The process of autophagy continues to occur, helping promote cellular repair and regeneration. This can lead to improvements in overall health and well-being. Around day six, most people begin to feel an enhanced sense of physical and mental well-being as cellular optimization occurs. Were you to break your fast at this stage, you would experience a heightened sense of taste and smell as sensory processing becomes more attuned with less energy expenditure during digestion. You may also experience even more focus and mental clarity with a potential for increased creativity.

Day Seven: Deeper Housecleaning and Revitalization

By the seventh day, inflammation in your body may start to decrease. Chronic inflammation is commonly linked to many diseases, such as heart disease, diabetes, and certain cancers. Fasting has been shown to have anti-inflammatory effects, which can help reduce your risk of these chronic diseases. As inflammation decreases, you may experience clearer, more radiant skin. This is because inflammation can contribute to skin issues like acne, eczema, and premature aging.

Day Eight: Hitting Your Stride

By the eighth day of your water fast, your digestive system is getting a much-needed break. Without the work of processing food, it can rest and repair itself. This can lead to improvements in digestive health and a reduction in issues like bloating, gas, and indigestion. Fasting also promotes the growth of beneficial gut bacteria, which play a crucial role in proper digestion, nutrient absorption, and immune function.

Day Nine: The Peak of Fasting

By the ninth day, your body's insulin sensitivity may improve more. When you consume a diet high in processed foods and sugar, your cells can become resistant to insulin, leading to high blood-sugar levels and an increased risk of type 2 diabetes. Fasting has been shown to drastically and dramatically improve insulin sensitivity, which means your cells become more responsive to insulin's signals. This can help lower your blood-sugar levels and reduce your risk of developing insulin resistance.

Day Ten: Feeling Your Best

As you reach this milestone, your body has undergone significant changes. Your cells have been repaired and regenerated through the process of autophagy, your inflammation levels have decreased, and your insulin sensitivity has improved. You may also notice improvements in your mental well-being, such as reduced stress and anxiety and increased feelings of calm and clarity. Fasting has been shown to have positive effects on brain health, including the growth of new brain cells and the protection of existing ones.[8]

BEYOND TEN DAYS

Beyond the first ten days is my favorite part of the fast, as everyone who perseveres through the turbulence to this point feels a sense of physical lightness and resilience. You feel your spirit, soul, and body in alignment and experience emotional clarity and shifts in self-perception. There is no dissonance in your prayer and meditation times, and your spiritual awareness and connection is unparalleled. Petty things don't seem to bother you as much, and you always walk with a song in your soul. There is also an increased sensitivity to physical sensa-tions and all sensory stimuli. I don't know how else to describe it, but it's almost as though the colors around you get brighter and you can smell everything.

To give you an idea of what to expect for longer fasts, what follows is the high-level, macro perspective of the changes your body will experience.

Days Eleven to Thirteen: Reaching a Deeper Metabolic State

With continued fasting, your body is firmly established in ke-tosis. Fat metabolism is optimized, and ketones are keeping your body fueled efficiently. Autophagy persists, contributing to ongoing cellular rejuvenation and repair. However, this stage also introduces new challenges and opportunities.

HORMONAL SHIFTS

Longer-term hormonal adaptations start to occur. Decreased insulin sensitivity and increased production of human growth hormone (HGH) can increase both fat-burning and cellular repair. Some individuals might experience changes in body-temperature regulation due to metabolic adaptations. If I can conjure up a word to describe the feelings that separate this state from the earlier phases, it would be the word *grounded*. You would have just come through a season of the most spo-radic shifts and changes in emotions and feelings, and in this phase, the feeling of sublime joy and tranquility feels more sustained.

PHYSICAL CHANGES

You may notice continued weight loss and visible changes in body composition. Some people report increased flexibility and a looser feeling in their skin due to decreased inflammation and cellular-waste removal. People also tend to experience changes in body-temperature regulation.

MENTAL AND EMOTIONAL STATE

Feelings of heightened mental clarity persist. However, depending on individual responses, this period might also bring a sense of introspection or emotional sensitivity. Dreams may become more vivid and unusual.

Days Fourteen to Fifteen: Adaptation and Renewal

By the end of the second week of fasting, the body has undergone significant metabolic and cellular changes. While weight loss continues, it often slows down as the body reaches a more balanced state of utilizing stored energy and conserving resources.

IMMUNE MODULATION

Some studies suggest that extended fasting can stimulate stem-cell activity and might have positive effects on immune-system function.[9]

SPIRITUAL AND PSYCHOLOGICAL IMPACT

This highly individualistic stage can bring about feelings of profound transformation and insight. For some people, extended fasting provides a sense of spiritual cleansing or connection.

A FEW NOTES FOR LONG FASTS

The challenge for some individuals is that once they become aware of the benefits, spiritual high, and mental clarity of fasting, they decide to double up, using the "more is more" logic, and extend their fasts. But after the compound benefits of extended fasting, you reach a point not just of diminishing returns but of potential danger to your body. Remember, it is not recommended to fast for overly extended times, and certainly not beyond forty days. Beyond forty days, the body shifts into starvation mode, which can lead to lasting harm.

Everyone's fasting experience is deeply personal and incredibly unique. The timeline I just provided varies based on numerous factors like preexisting health conditions, body composition, and mental state. All these factors influence the physiological changes and how someone feels during a fast. For example, if you have a high-carb, high-sugar diet, most of those processes won't start until a few days in, as your body must burn through all its glucose before your insulin can level down. Once it comes down, it kick-starts the processes mentioned, and the body can begin to switch fuel sources.

MEDICAL SUPERVISION

Water fasts beyond a few days should ideally be undertaken with medical supervision to monitor for potential complications and ensure safety. I would suggest you speak with your doctor to discuss the health implications specific to you. It may be beneficial to also let your doctor know that fasting is something you will be doing periodically moving forward, as, like prayer, it is a lifestyle and not an event.

There are also considerable risks to be mindful of while engaging in a water fast. Electrolyte imbalances become more critical, and close monitoring is recommended. It's crucial to do fasting with accountability and in community, listen to your body's signals for anything abnormal, and seek medical consultation if needed.

My brother Thando called me one day at the end of 2020 and told me that his body was breaking down because he was on various diabetes and blood-pressure medications that had severely diminished his quality of life. He was asking me to pray for him. I immediately told him what I had learned from extensive research on fasting, which indicated that high blood pressure is not necessarily an acquired disease but the body's response to a misaligned system. I told Thando that his body was working overtime and that although the medication was keeping him alive, it was also inhibiting him from living. I challenged him to a twenty-one-day fast that I would do with him, and I committed to explaining what was happening to his body at every turn. This meant (as you could probably tell from the breakdown we just did of days one through ten) that a lot of acute changes happened in his body, resulting at first in pain and discomfort. At times, his mind was convinced his body was dying, but as we have already established, that was simply the body's mechanism to jolt him back into his previous state of caloric intake. This cognitive dissonance was not unique to him but rather was relatively standard for one's first serious foray into an extended water fast. Today my brother is very much alive, well, and missing a hundred pounds of literal deadweight because of the incredible gift of fasting. His spirit is lighter now, and his ability to hear God has drastically increased.

God is a good God and a *great* Father, and He would not have directed us to the ancient paths and this beautiful practice if it were dangerous, deadly, or meant to punish or harm us. Fasting is truly an intimate and life-changing journey of discovery with God, His Holy Spirit, and wisdom.

7

The Inner Battle

MOST PEOPLE LIKEN FASTING to running a marathon, but I prefer the battle analogy. When we decide to fast, our souls mount an internal assault—an all-out war—because going one, two, four, or even six weeks without any source of sustenance doesn't make much sense. That is why my greatest advice to people who want to start fasting is simply this: Just start and take it, as Jesus and that country singer said, "one day at a time."[1] I say that because as surely as I know anything to be true, once you start, you've won half the war.

For that first week, your mind will remind you of all the reasons it makes sense for you to quit. I've heard so many people tell me (and my own experience corroborates this) that it feels as though the entire universe is conspiring against you. You show up to work and your notoriously stingy boss has bought lunch for the team. You enter the break room and there are trays of free doughnuts—the good kind. Somebody baked you your favorite red-velvet cake, and that happens only when (and every single time) you fast. Not to come across as a cosmic conspiracy theorist, but there is an antithetical spiritual force that does not want to see you fast, let alone pray, and the battle for you to quit every day will feel quite real.

Don't be surprised to find that your inner dialogue takes on a more aggressive nature and that your most intimate thoughts will tell you how fruitless your fast is because you're not praying as much or you messed up and sinned, thought a thought, or did a deed. Each day, you must make a *determined,* nonnegotiable decision to stick to your fasting commitment, even if that's just for one more day. As we know from life in general and all things worth doing, it's a relentless commitment to keep on going, putting one foot in front of the other, that eventually finishes hikes, marathons, and what I believe to be the most redemptive use of our endurance, fasting. Our faith is built upon a foundation mixed with pain, hardship, and sorrow, yet I believe we have lost sight of the theology of suffering. Unfortunately, this has spawned indulgent ways of living and thinking. We've forgotten that some of the most challenging experiences bring the most good. Fasting strikes at the very root of this principle.

I want you to understand what is happening when you fast so you can temper your expectation. My primary-school teacher always had this catchphrase before giving us unsolicited wisdom: "Forewarned is forearmed."

FEELING SPIRITUAL?

Most people will say they feel less spiritual while fasting. They feel further from God, and they sense some of the old desires and habits start to raise their nasty heads. I would like to assure you that not only is this normal, but it's to be expected as well, if you are doing your fasting right. Remember, fasting is a purifying process. Much like the refining of silver, gold, and all precious metals, the intense heat is what brings up the impurities. It's the pressure that produces diamonds, and at the heart of fasting is a slow and refining sacrifice. For the first few fasting days, the soul (which includes the mind) will tell you you're dying in order to try to jump-start the ingestion process. After all, normal life (as your mind knows it) has completely changed. The flesh will agonizingly whisper, *You're doing it wrong. Might as well quit,* and your body will corroborate every one of those whispers with aches, pains, and hunger pangs. That is why it's imperative to stay anchored on the promises of God, His goodness, and your purpose for the fast. Your "why" is more powerful than you may realize, and keeping it firmly in the front of your mind will help immensely. Regularly refreshing your mindset with the Word will help ease your mental worries. It's also imperative to drink plenty of water, as many of the body's discomforts can be alleviated with proper hydration. With all the toxins being purged at a cellular level, you need to constantly stay hydrated to flush all the garbage out. Headaches and nausea during fasting are usually tied to overall bodily toxicity, and having a body in pain makes it increasingly tempting to quit. A personal rule of thumb for me is to try to double the recommended intake of eight glasses of water a day. Dr. Myles Munroe, in a popular You-Tube video, advises drinking a glass of water every time you feel a hunger pang.[2] I mostly agree with that, but water sometimes throws off the electrolyte balance for some people, so as long as you're taking electrolytes if you need to, then hydrate away.

One of the most comforting things is that as you say yes to fasting and take the first intentional step, the Holy Spirit and His grace come to meet your efforts, and what may not be easy becomes simple as you cooperate with Him. I have found that when fasting is done with surrender to and cooperation with the Holy Spirit, it becomes more transformational, less daunting, and easier to integrate as a rule of life. And the more you fast, the more you will develop a growing awareness of your body's unique fasting idiosyncrasies and learn to discern how your fasting is going based on experience and repetition. I call that building fasting muscle memory. By God's grace, fasting, like every other discipline, can be matured and mastered over time for phenomenal health benefits and incredible spiritual growth.

SURRENDERING TO DISCIPLINE

Most of us fixate on the discomfort of fasting, especially if we haven't yet experienced how these challenges are rendered irrelevant within the first three days of fasting because of the incredible way God made our chemistry. I love drawing the parallel of the annihilation of the old and resurrection of the new after the third day. Fasting tears down before it builds up. Especially in the initial stages, there is an acute affliction of our senses that needs to be accompanied by an unrelenting trust in the process. No matter the pain, we trust and power through, and His grace, as expressed through our bodies, meets us at the point of weakness. That is one of my favorite things about this incredible practice. So much of our faith walk is simulated and, consequently, learned in our embracing of it. I like what one of my favorite teachers and one of the most devoted fasting fans I know, Stacie Wood, says about it: "Fasting is the only discipline I know that teaches by what it takes."

So true! Trust the process. Trust a good Father and His heart and His design of all your faculties. You were intricately designed for His pleasure and glory, and every calibration tool He gives you on your journey to a life lived in total conformity and communion with His Son is good. Ultimately good. Objectively good.

Now, I say objectively good because it won't always feel that way. My young son has recently developed a mean and determined streak of not only rejecting but also fighting against everything we deem good for him. Baby vitamins when he's sick, washing his hands, eating his vegetables, wiping his face, changing his diaper—anything other than him picking up random things and putting them in his mouth is a fight. In his immaturity, he believes what feels good *to* him is good *for* him, but we know how far from the truth that is. The following is one of my favorite scriptures, and it accurately describes what our disposition should be toward fasting:

> Endure hardship as discipline; God is treating you as his children. For what children are not disciplined by their father? If you are not disciplined—and everyone undergoes discipline—then you are not legitimate, not true sons and daughters at all. . . .
>
> God disciplines us for our good, in order that we may share in his holiness. *No discipline seems pleasant at the time, but painful. Later, however, it produces a harvest of righteousness and peace for those who have been trained by it.*
>
> Therefore, strengthen your feeble arms and weak knees. "Make level paths for your feet," so that the lame may not be disabled, but rather healed. (Hebrews 12:7–8, 10–13, NIV, emphasis added)

When we allow the discipline of fasting to train us and produce something truly valuable in and through us, it brings peace and a life that is rightly aligned. The path to freedom is always found within the parameters of discipline. We know that if we want to live longer, we must eat healthily, sleep well, and exercise regularly. Each of these *good* things is at the same time a rejection of its opposite, yet this kind of discipline leads to more energy, life, and freedom in the end. Such is the same both in the spirit and in life. The entryway is always narrow, and once we embrace the discomfort the narrowing of discipline brings, we will live our lives mostly free of the pain of constriction and regret. I believe that's what the Hebrews 12 passage means when it speaks of setting straight paths for our feet, creating a narrowing rule that allows vaster lives and keeps us moving toward true freedom.

I love how evangelist Andrew Murray once described the correlation and interplay between fasting and prayer: "Prayer is the one hand with which we grasp the invisible; fasting, the other, with which we let loose and cast away the visible."[3]

Fasting, at the core of its potency, primarily recalibrates our perspective. The wrestling between what's natural and supernatural exists primarily in the mind (a faculty of the soul), and when we fast, we can truly begin to see the spiritual realm more clearly, like the lifting of a morning fog.

That is why fasting isn't simply abstinence from food. It is much more than that. Fasting is an ancient and highly effective spiritual practice. It's been known, used, and trusted in every major religion and culture and is a practice that the fathers of our faith—and our Lord Himself—relied on. It's the only practice I know of that touches all three faculties, as it empowers the spirit, engages the soul, and benefits the body. As someone once told me in casual conversation, "A diet changes the way we look, but fasting changes the way we see." Truer words could not be spoken.

DEEPENING OUR COMMUNION WITH GOD THROUGH PRAYER

God has given us incredible tools, practices, and disciplines to help our whole beings on our journey of maturing into Christ-likeness. Fasting is a preparatory tool that helps us pray as we ought to. In fact, fasting is never really mentioned in the Bible outside the context of prayer. In humbling our souls (our reasoning agents), fasting elevates our spirits, through which we commune and communicate with God.

There is truly a grace for prayer released when we fast. The discipline I stretched myself to learn and protect throughout each fast is to pray for two hours each day. Most people brought up in faith households in the African context (myself included) are trained to pray an hour in the morning and an hour at night, based on Jesus's humble rebuke to His disciples in Matthew 26:40: "Could you not watch with Me one hour?"

I have noticed that when I'm fasting, praying feels simple and the flow is effortless. It's not infrequent that I will pray beyond the allotted two hours. It's evident that in those moments, my spirit is praying without the interference and distractions of the soul.

Now, that does not mean building the stamina to pray this long is easy. Prayer and fasting are simple but not always easy. You start by deciding to show up and do the hard work, consistently. Your prayer muscle is built the same way your physical muscles are built in the gym: incrementally, daily being pushed past the previous limits.

The way I was culturally taught was to start by praying for fifteen minutes, divided into three five-minute phases. The logic behind this was simply that *anyone* can pray for fifteen minutes. Building endurance is made a bit easier when you focus on three practices in prayer: thanksgiving, petition, and intercession. Each of these practices have parallels with the biblical temple and our tripartite makeup.

Thanksgiving (Outer Courts and the Body)

I would always begin my prayer time with thanksgiving. This prayer practice is represented by the outer courts in the temple. With thanksgiving, we cross the threshold into God's presence. The psalmist lays this out for us: "Enter into His gates with thanksgiving" (Psalm 100:4).

How else do you approach a good, loving, and wise king who has given us all things that pertain to life and godliness, as 2 Peter 1:3 reminds us? In this initial phase, nothing is too small. I thank God for a meal I enjoyed or an interaction I found particularly kind. I thank Him for my clothes, His provision, and my friends and family. I thank Him for that parking spot, my health, that pimple that cleared overnight—everything and all things. Remember, God is a Father, and with great fathers and their kids, the heart and posture of gratitude is what matters.

My mother used an old hymn called "Count Your Blessings" to remind us to "name them one by one."[4] The practice of thankfulness not only prepares us for a lifelong disposition of gratitude, a most beautiful virtue, but also conditions us for the next part (petition), which is the next five minutes of our prayer practice.

You may find it challenging to remember things to be thankful for after the first minute, but stick with it. You might get bored, but I've found boredom in prayer to usually come from a wandering mind, so perhaps bringing paper and a pen into your prayer time will help ground your thoughts.

Another hack my wife uses is keeping a gratitude journal. She goes through the day actively looking for moments of God's favor and goodness in her life and writes them down. Later, she prays through the list with gratitude. It's no wonder she is one of the most joyful and faith-filled people I know.

Petition (Inner Courts and the Soul)

From thanksgiving, we progress into the inner court of prayer, where we pray for the things we would love to be thankful for. This is where we make our personal requests known to God.

In the temple, the inner courts were where the priests carried out the daily rituals. In light of that, I look at this time in prayer as the time to pray about all the things that I, as a son, would ask a good Father. I ask God for forgiveness where it's needed—for Him to align my heart with His. I ask Him to bless my marriage. I ask Him to protect my son. I ask for His favor in the work I do. I ask Him for His grace over my finances.

The previous hack of using a list also applies here. I petition for five minutes before I move on to the final phase of my prayer time, and that is intercession.

Intercession (Holy of Holies and the Spirit)

As the Holy of Holies was the most inner and sacred place in the temple, and our spirits are the innermost centers of ourselves, intercession is the most intimate place of prayer. This stage has nothing to do with us and everything to do with the Lord. It is where we ask for *His* burdens and intercede over them with His Spirit. I believe that the heart of true intercession is when we ask the Lord what is on His heart—what friends, cities, people, groups, situations—and then ask Him to intervene on their behalf. This is the most interactive phase, as we listen and then pray. After all, prayer is mutual communion between us and the Lord, speaking and listening. In this posture, the Holy Spirit, the glorious teacher, prompts our spirits with directions for what we should pray for.

Building the Practice

The following simple guideline is great for building this practice of prayer: Start with fifteen minutes total (for all three phases of prayer combined). Do that for two days, and then add two minutes to each phase for a total of twenty-one minutes. Why wait two days? The way my mother explained it to me was that the first day is for pushing past your limit, and the next is for proving that the first time wasn't a fluke. Continue this two-day growth cadence until each phase of prayer lasts twenty-one minutes, totaling a little more than an hour.

Now, this is a template, and once the guardrails are in place and the practice secure in your daily regimen, you may notice the Holy Spirit begin to tweak the ratio as you feel Him wanting to linger in one phase over the other. Follow His lead. He is, after all, the Lord of your devotion. Sometimes we let guardrails become jail cells, and what should have been convention becomes constricting. Once again, everyone's walk is different—beautiful and sacred. And God is faithful and good to lead each one of us further into His holy presence.

8

After the Fast

THE MOST COMMON QUESTIONS I'm asked once people begin a fast are always these two: "How do I know it's time to break the fast, and how do I break it?" Now, I'm not necessarily talking about people who may have the duration of their fast set to a specific number of days, the most popular being fasts lasting seven, fourteen, twenty-one, or forty days (the latter for the blessed overachievers). These are usually milestone fasts, where you endure until you reach the allocated number of days the Lord may have called you to or that you have set based on your schedule and capacity. It matters not which. Once the number of days is set, commit yourself fully and go for it. The Lord's grace will sustain you through your fast.

There are, however, people who begin longer—or what we call open-ended—fasts, in which the individual, much like when running a marathon, keeps going with the fast until either the body tells them to stop or there is a disruption in their devotion or schedule, at which point they gracefully bow out. If you find yourself in an open-ended fast or maybe in your zeal had set a lofty extended goal but now find yourself (in conjunction with medical and sound communal counsel) unable to continue, what I'm about to share is how you know it's time to break that fast. Although, I strongly suggest you take bowing out of your fast into serious consideration only after what I call the equilibrium mark.

What is this equilibrium mark, and how do we know we have hit it? Remember my previous analogy of the bodily processes during fasting like being on an airplane during a severe thunderstorm? There is a strong initial system shock where the higher you climb, the more it seems as though everything around you is falling apart. All imaginable alarms and beepers are going off. I know, that is a very dramatic analogy, but being in the middle of a tumultuous fast can feel that way sometimes. Your entire body is in shock because you suddenly stopped feeding all your addictions, so your sugar, caffeine, alcohol, entertainment, and whatever other fix of choice are instantaneously clamoring for attention and demanding your instant recidivism. Much like any functional addict, you will find yourself in the clutches of the most severe withdrawals, so your brain is discombobulated by intense cravings, you are drenched in a cold sweat, you have a head-splitting migraine, and your body cannot stop shivering. That, by the way, is no exaggeration: It was how I felt on the eighth day of my first-ever extended twenty-one-day fast. I went into literal withdrawals!

In all candor, this was simply because I was a thirty-five-year-old man who, in the words of a colleague of mine, had the eating habits of a teenager. I drank sodas copiously at every meal, the main offender being the legendary Dr Pepper. I was also a snob with this one, because my preferred libation was the *Dublin* Dr Pepper, which is the somewhat rare bottled version named after Dublin, Texas, near where Dr Pepper was created. This blessed variant of the revered king of sodas uses real cane sugar and tastes heavenly. If it was not in supply, then the bottled Mexican Coke (with real sugar) was my next go-to. It had to be the big bottle, though, because . . . why not? Everything is bigger in Texas. Speaking of Texas, I was a BBQ connoisseur in Dallas, a shameless carnivore whose every meal consisted of some form of red meat. I also had an insatiable sweet tooth and used to churn my own ice cream with a machine I "invested in" (as I told my wife) after my faithful purchases had undoubtedly pushed up Blue Bell Creameries stock a few indices over the years. Because I'd been blessed with great genetics, I could get away with those eating habits without love handles making an appearance. So it's absolutely no wonder that when I decided to fast, my entire body had a full-on war on its hands. My detox phase took four severe days, and had I not known what was happening, I would have broken the fast and sought medical help. But the beauty of knowledge enabled me to coach myself through. I told myself, *I know it hurts, but keep pushing. Keep going. You're almost there. The adverse effects are only temporary, and the outcome will be redemptive.* The true beauty of the human body, soul, and spirit is that we will endure almost anything and everything if we know that the pain is temporary and the outcome will be beautifully redemptive.

My prayer over this book and this resource is that it will serve as an encouraging guide that will help you know that whatever is happening to you is just a normal (albeit painful) part of the process and you will come out as pure gold on the other side. Job 23:10 illustrates this: "He knows the way that I take; when He has tested me, I shall come forth as gold." I've also found Psalm 66:11–12 to perfectly capture not just the painful complexity of the process but also to be a helpful philosophy for me to anchor my mind and heart upon:

> You brought us into the net;
>> you laid a crushing burden on our backs;
> you let men ride over our heads;
>> we went through fire and through water;
>> yet you have brought us out to a place of abundance.
>
> (ESV)

FASTING PRODUCES RESILIENCE

Fasting is a hard discipline. It's an intentional death on the altar of sacrifice, because as we mentioned before, spiritually, physically, and emotionally, you are undergoing an active death of sorts, at a cellular level, with scientific proof to boot.[1] Much like Jesus in the garden, you are being willfully crushed through the purifying crucible of suffering, knowing that it's only for the joy that lies before you that you can withstand the discomfort and pain and lean into the press, much like grapes that have to die to produce premium vintage.

A contemporary concept that has been gaining traction in recent years is one called antifragility, developed by the mathematical statistician Nassim Nicholas Taleb and outlined in his seminal book *Antifragile: Things That Gain from Disorder*. Antifragility refers to systems that improve in capability when exposed to stressors, shocks, volatility, uncertainty, mistakes, attacks, or failures.[2] This concept states that unlike mere resilience, in which an individual responds to stressors with the goal of returning to its original form with minimal impact to its core structure or functions, *antifragile systems* thrive and grow in response to challenges. Taleb points to the clearest example of that in nature, and I would even subjectively bring it closer to home in the form of our very physiology. How do you build muscle in the gym? You introduce stressors, or controlled chaos, into your muscles that tear your muscle tissue, and after resting, the tissue builds back much stronger. We understand that trials and tragedy make for better, more-grounded individuals. Much like salt in any culinary undertaking, pain truly adds dimensionality to our otherwise tepid existences. I believe it's the same principle of growth in horticulture, such as when Jesus, in John 15:2, reminds us that any branch that bears fruit is pruned so that it may bear more fruit. It's also the same principle found in John 12:24: "Unless a grain of wheat falls into the ground and dies, it remains alone; but if it dies, it produces much grain."

The path to growth, maturity, and multiplication in any system (nature being a true witness) is through the path of pain and pruning. This simple concept is so embedded into the dynamics and DNA of all living things that not even Jesus, divine deity and the creator of all living things, could escape it. Hebrews 5:7–9 gives us a movingly personal perspective into this:

> In the days of his flesh, Jesus offered up prayers and supplications, with loud cries and tears, to him who was able to save him from death, and he was heard because of his reverence. Although he was a son, he learned obedience through what he suffered. And being made perfect, he became the source of eternal salvation to all who obey him. (ESV)

Jesus learned obedience through pain, agonized cries, tears, and suffering and emerged as the source of eternal salvation. Isn't that true, though, that whenever we go through something both traumatic and transformational, we always emerge with an irrefutable authority to speak into said situation? So, yes, fasting is hard, painful, and excruciating, but it is truly the most holistically transformational undertaking you will ever engage in, as there is such an undergirding grace available to us as we carry this cross.

As with any discipline, fasting does get easier after you have made it a consistent practice on your discipleship journey. But until then, the first few times you fast, your body will fall apart and you may sleep in pain and discomfort, only to wake up into the most tangibly peaceful and vibrant reality you have ever experienced. That is the equilibrium I was referring to. Once you have gone through the adverse effects of your bodily processes actively detoxing and rectifying your compromised systems, everything stabilizes and you wake up with more clarity and peace than you thought possible.

Most of the time when we think of peace, we think of a sublime, muted existence where all things exist in quiet harmony, but that's not fully what I'm trying to convey. This peace is unlike any other experience.

That equilibrium hit me on the morning of day thirteen of my fast, but as I mentioned before, your experience will vary based on your eating habits pre-fast. I woke up and could *feel* the peace. I felt incredible presence of mind and a mental clarity and a focus no medication can give. No lag. No grogginess. All systems instantaneously firing and working together like one coherent unit. I felt a sustained energy that didn't ebb and flow during the day. An example I sometimes give is that it's like driving a Tesla after a lifetime of driving internal combustion engines. When you floor the accelerator, the power is delivered instantly, and you revel in this strange yet new and glorious experience as the sheer force nails you to the back of your seat. Pure adrenaline! That's what the equilibrium-state-induced-energy dispersion feels like when fasting. I remember thinking, *Wow, this is what the detoxed, emancipated body is meant to feel like.* A flawless, powerful, meticulously tuned engine. Hardware and software functioning as one coherent, inextricable unit. If for no other reason, do an extended fast just to feel that feeling. It will cost you to get there, but I can assure you, you have never felt anything like it!

WHEN TO BREAK THE FAST

So, when do you know it's time to break an open-ended or extended fast? Simply, it's when your hunger returns.

Remember that during the onset stages of your fast, usually around the second or third day (varying based on your pre-fast diet and how much glucose is stored and how quickly your body can burn through it and shift energy sources), your hunger disappears the moment your body hits ketosis (switches its fuel source to ketones). That is because ketones are hunger suppressants; therefore, you don't feel hunger from that moment on. As your fast continues, the body uses autophagy and stored fat for energy, but once these stores are all but depleted, the body will once again reintroduce hunger into the system to jump-start the digestive process. For my very first fast, that happened at day twenty, and because I was so close to my end date, I persevered. Along with the physical hunger returning, your mind switches from that sublime state of peace, focus, and communion with the Lord to intense cravings and thoughts of food—all methods the body uses to remind you that it's time to eat.

Some people push past that sign and go longer, and when that happens, the body gets a second wind of sorts and begins the process all over, this time burning muscle mass for fuel. I don't recommend such a prolonged fast unless the Lord has specifically called you to it, in which case you'd have, along with His call, the grace to sustain it. Otherwise, you will be extremely miserable and put your body in medical jeopardy. I have a few friends who have water fasted forty days and they corroborate the challenges of going beyond the twenty-one-day mark. Multiple people, from Jesus to Moses, did it, but the divine call, and consequent grace, is evident in all their narratives.

The key to being a successful and consistent faster is learning to listen to and know what your body is saying and what processes are normal for the number of days you have been fasting. Everything, from your body to your mind to the devil, has a voice and a very strong opinion when you fast, which is why having a resource like this book, listening to fasting sermons and podcasts, and making yourself accountable to people who have fasted longer than you are keys to doing it safely and effectively. Remember, though, discomfort or even pain during a fast is not uncommon but rather is, in most cases, an indicator that transformation is happening at a cellular level.

Trust the process, lean into the grace of God, and persevere. He would never give us one of His most meaningful practices and pair it with the most sacred of communion in prayer if it were hazardous to our health or destructive to His temples, which are our bodies.

As painful as the whip cleansing of His Father's temple was, Jesus rained it down on the money changers. The result was a cleansed and much more efficient temple. In the same way, let this blessed practice remove all the toxins, disease, and cancerous growths from your bodily temple and optimize your soul to do the Master's will.

HOW TO BREAK THE FAST

This topic is a very important one. There are numerous narratives of people who ran into all sorts of health complications after breaking an extended fast the wrong way, and I personally know of two who lost their lives.

Breaking your fast well is as important as starting it. Your entire body would have, at this point, acclimated to an optimized fuel source, your digestive system would basically be in hibernation, and extreme caution must be exercised in reintroducing food back into your body.

But first I would like to talk about the spiritual posture that should happen before the bodily process of ending your fast.

Gratitude

The first thing to remember is the spiritual reason you initially embarked on the fast. I know that the bodily health benefits speak for themselves, but think about the spiritual "why" to your fast. Some people fast because they are praying and hoping for a miracle, and others because of a desire for devotion and nearness to the Lord. Some fast for the wisdom and counsel of hearing God clearly over a particular situation, and nothing I know of quiets the soul and attunes our hearts and hearing to the voice of God and the whispers of His Spirit like fasting.

Whatever the case, we keep that reason front and center to the whole process as we fast. Think of Queen Esther fasting when the genocidal Haman threatened her whole nation with extinction (see Esther 3). Think of King David as he fasted with sackcloth and ashes and pleaded for God to spare the life of his illegitimately conceived son (see 2 Samuel 12:16). There was a singular path and focus to their seeking God with prayer and fasting, and I have found that kind of focus to be such an anchoring virtue during extended fasts.

The fringe benefit of singular focus is that we know beyond the shadow of a doubt that our prayers have been heard by God and we can rejoice fully over the answers we receive. John 16:24 reads, "Until now you have asked nothing in My name. Ask, and you will receive, that your joy may be full." So as you begin to approach the finish line, switch your prayer to thanksgiving.

I usually spend the last two days of every fast thanking the Lord for two primary things, the first being His grace. Going in depth into a fast makes you acutely aware of how only the grace of God could have helped you accomplish such a supernatural feat and complex bodily process. Chances are, you had divine encounters, moments of clarity, and assurances of God's presence during the fast, and an acute awareness of His pleasure over you. Thank Him for that. Whatever your fasting journey entailed, the appropriate response is gratitude and worship.

In those last two days, I replay all the moments when I encountered His nearness during the fast, the times He gave me the gift of revelation in His Word, or even the moments I felt my heart tender toward Him, and I just thank Him. The ultimate reward in any context is the pleasure of God with us. I then thank Him for the specific answers to my petitions, whether I received them during the fast or not.

In my many fasts, there have been only a handful of times when I received a breakthrough or the desired outcome during the actual fast. Most of the time, the answers came after the fast, and I have found that to be the experience for most people. Remember, God still reigns sovereign over the answer and the timing of its manifestation. Our role is simply to cry out and seek Him in desperation and trust His divine response and sovereign timing.

Listening

The second thing to remember when breaking a fast is to listen. Your spirit will be at its most sensitive at the end of your fast. That is also the time when your tripartite being will be at its most harmonious, so spend moments listening. Silently bring your mind to focus and ask the Lord to speak to you. Ask Him to speak about your friends, your family, and even your finances. That is not necessarily asking for more things but rather simply echoing these words of young Samuel: "Speak, for Your servant hears" (1 Samuel 3:10). Sometimes the Lord speaks, but I always take comfort in the simple and grounding truth that my petitions and desires were at least heard by the creator of all things. That is enough. All else is a plus.

REINTRODUCING FOOD

Let's shift to the practical aspects of breaking the fast, pertinent to our physiology. When it's time to begin refeeding, what do we eat, when, and why?

It usually takes me only a week to fully adjust back to regular eating, but most people take about two. I believe that can fluctuate based on the sensitivity of each person's digestive system. You can never go wrong with planning on the adjustment taking longer, but let a week be the minimum you allow yourself. Taking less than a week is highly discouraged.

Breaking a twenty-one-day water fast requires a gradual and cautious approach to avoid overwhelming your digestive system and causing potential harm. Following is a detailed fifteen-day guide on how to safely break an extended water fast, along with the physiological reasoning behind each step.

DAYS ONE TO THREE POST-FAST: REINTRODUCE LIQUIDS INTO YOUR DIET

You have to start small. If you go straight to a juicy steak or something else you were craving, you will very likely throw it up, and that's assuming that your constricted digestive tract would allow it into your stomach to begin with. Your palate has been completely reset and you can literally taste every ounce of salt and artificial additive.

By the way, I find a renewed palate to be one of my favorite things about breaking a fast. Your taste buds are alive, so every bite is a burst of flavor! Start with a single grape or one bite into a slice of watermelon. I remember the first time I ate a grape post-fast and thought, *So, this is what a grape truly tastes like!* All the nuance and complex notes in the flavor. It's truly an amazing sensation! Grapes aside, the following are the liquids I would recommend, starting with what I believe is the first and best thing to consume when breaking a fast: bone broth.

Day One: Bone Broth

Start with small sips of bone broth throughout the day. It is rich in electrolytes and easily digestible amino acids, gently easing your gut back into processing nutrients. It also helps replenish electrolytes lost during fasting and tastes delicious. Sips only, though. Don't make a meal of it yet or you risk bringing it all back up again.

Day Two: Diluted Juices

Gradually introduce diluted vegetable or fruit juices such as that of carrots, cucumbers, and watermelon. These provide vitamins, minerals, and natural sugars without overloading your system. Stick to just the juice at this point. Your body can't handle the fiber yet.

Day Three: Herbal Teas

Sip on decaffeinated herbal teas to stay hydrated and soothe your digestive system. Avoid sugary or dairy-based options. Introducing coffee may give you an irritated stomach due to the caffeine, so I would just stick to decaffeinated teas. I have found milk thistle a phenomenal tea supplement to help the liver and kidneys further cleanse and detox. They have been hard at work, and this tea helps lift a little of their burden. Another pleasant decaffeinated tea with incredible antioxidant properties to drink post-fast is rooibos, a red South African tea with a pleasant, distinct taste and aroma. I would recommend you add it to your fast-breaking routine.

DAYS FOUR TO SEVEN: EXPAND TO SOFT FOODS

Day Four: Fermented Foods

Begin introducing small portions of fermented foods such as yogurt, kefir, and sauerkraut. These contain beneficial bacteria that aid digestion and replenish your gut microbiome, which may have been affected by the fast.

Day Five: Soft Solids

This is when we begin the gradual reintroduction of soft solids. Incorporate easily digestible steamed vegetables such as broccoli, cauliflower, and carrots. Start with small quantities and gradually increase them as your body tolerates.

Days Six and Seven: Light Soups

Enjoy light vegetable soups and pureed ones made from non-starchy vegetables. These provide essential nutrients and hydration without overwhelming your digestive system.

DAYS EIGHT TO FOURTEEN: GRADUALLY REINTRODUCE MORE VARIETY

Gradually, over the next week, begin to incorporate the following food groups. Start with small servings, and then slowly build up to larger portions over the span of a few days.

Fruits

This is where the feeding fun begins. Your body will be craving fruit, so start incorporating low-sugar fruits such as berries, apples, and pears. These provide vitamins, fiber, and natural sweetness.

Whole Grains

Introduce small portions of cooked whole grains such as brown rice and quinoa. These provide complex carbohydrates for sustained energy. At this point, you will begin feeling more like yourself as far as energy goes. Granted, if your refeeding process tracks along a bit faster than two weeks, this will happen much sooner.

Legumes

Add cooked lentils and beans to your diet for additional protein and fiber.

DAY FIFTEEN ONWARD: TRANSITION TO A BALANCED DIET

Gradually reintroduce a balanced diet of whole foods, lean protein, healthy fats, and complex carbohydrates. Avoid processed foods, excess sugar, and large meals as your body continues to readjust.

Be very vigilant, though, because the body will want to recoup its losses and cause you to go into a feeding frenzy. Most people fall into this trap and end up with worse eating habits and more weight than when they started, so exercise extreme caution and absolute diligence in maintaining a healthy, balanced, and temperate diet post-fast.

Think of the fast not as a moratorium from your questionable eating habits but as a divine intervention for your body temple. It is your chance to reevaluate your eating habits and make intentional healthy choices. Don't go back and entangle yourself in the eating habits that held you in bondage. Any addiction to salt, oil, or sugar from this moment on will be completely voluntary because the fast will have depleted the cravings. You may miss the taste of said things, but they don't have a hold over you anymore, so walk in that freedom over your appetite.

Here are a few physiological considerations to note:

- During a fast, the production of digestive enzymes decreases. Therefore, reintroducing food slowly allows your body to ramp up enzyme production, preventing digestive discomfort.
- Fasting improves insulin sensitivity. Breaking the fast gradually helps maintain that sensitivity and avoids blood-sugar spikes.
- Fasting can alter your gut microbiome. Introducing fermented foods and fiber-rich ones helps restore a healthy balance of gut bacteria.
- It is imperative that you listen to your body throughout the process. If you experience any discomfort, slow down the reintroduction of food and consult a healthcare professional if necessary.
- If your body isn't very sensitive, the whole process can be condensed and you can be back to eating a normal diet in as little as a week. (Sooner than that is not recommended.) The process for breaking an extended fast is just as crucial as the fast itself, so patience and a steady, thoughtful, and gradual reintroduction of food are key to a successful and healthy transition back to normal eating.

FASTING AS A WAY OF LIFE

Now that you have successfully completed your fast, what's next? If it is truly to be a practice, how often should you do these extended fasts?

The first encouragement for your post-fast journey is simply this: Fasting is not an event but a lifestyle, much like prayer, worship, meditation, and the reading of the Word. Jesus clearly says that in Matthew 6:16–18 as He speaks to a culture that understands that. "*When* you fast . . ." Notice how He doesn't go into the logistics of fasting, as it was built into their culture. Our question beyond this point shouldn't be *if* you should fast but rather, as this book is titled, *how* to fast.

Fasting is meant to be a natural part of your lifestyle.

Remember, fasting is a tool to help you focus spiritually. It's a recalibrating tool for the soul, and a regenerative tool for the body. And all the benefits are most effective when used consistently. So don't just introduce fasting to your retinue of helpful practices that guide you on your journey of Christlikeness, but also make it the foundation. A lifestyle that incorporates fasting will keep your spirit, soul, and body in optimum shape, fit for the Master's good use.

Here are some practical ways I've seen this practice of fasting effectively and sustainably integrated into a lifestyle.

Weekly Cadence

I have found a seamless match for my life cadence by simply building a day of fasting into the rhythm of my weekly Sabbath. The Sabbath is supposed to be a time of rest, reflection, and consecration, which are all central to the ethos of fasting. I usually fast during the day and then break my fast in the company of friends, relatives, and loved ones in the evening. My schedule does not always allow me to do that, though, but I'm relentlessly intentional in trying to protect my routine. The clarity and calmness I find when fasting only compounds my rest and enjoyment of God and His creation on the Sabbath.

Weekly fasts seem to work best on the weekends. I have found that most people have more control over their schedules during the weekends. I also love that when I'm fasting and seeking or enjoying the Lord during the weekend, it also serves as a way to ground the past week and commit the upcoming week to the Lord. As a general rule, during my fast, I like to focus my attention on areas in my life where my prayers have not gone before and prepared the way for me. I *desperately* need to hear God's voice and direction in my day-to-day, as any decision I'm invited to make can have deep implications on my future and the Lord's ministry. As He has made me a steward of some influence, I've found that honor and responsibility accompanied by many opportunities to step into spaces and do things. Anything not birthed from God and His purposes for my life usually lacks His grace and empowerment, and those always give me untold headaches. So I have learned to be still, hear and heed the voice of my Shepherd and say only what He speaks, work only where He has finished working, and move only where He moves me. My greatest peace is in knowing that I am simply a pawn on the giant chessboard of His design and that I move, conquer, and advance at His pleasure and for His purpose. In this day and age of technological advancements that give anyone with two thumbs and an opinion a platform and considerable influence, the church has, unfortunately, lost a lot of credibility through speaking when the Lord has not. Never has there been a higher premium on sanctified ears being quick to hear and sanctified lips being slow to speak. Yet nothing sanctifies quicker than fasting, so stay with it.

Intermittent Fasting

Intermittent fasting is when you structure your food cadence into fasting and feeding windows. For example, a popular intermittent-fasting schedule is the 16:8, where, within a twenty-four-hour period, you fast for sixteen hours and eat meals only within an eight-hour window. A more extreme version of this is the 20:4, where all feeding happens within a four-hour window.

I have found intermittent fasting to be incredibly beneficial to both my body and my spirit as a primer for my actual fasts. Let me explain. Remember, the hurt and difficulty of extended fasting will always be directly proportional to your dietary habits prior to the fast. If you insist on returning to a high-SOS (salt, oil, sugar) diet after every fast, you will always hate fasting, as it will be difficult every single time. The headaches, detox, and withdrawals will always mark the early days of your fast (which are your most productive days, as that's when you have the most energy for fervent prayer) and not make for a pleasant experience. Your neurochemistry will then associate fasting with pain and discomfort and you will naturally want to avoid it, making a fasted lifestyle even more complicated.

But when you live an intermittently fasted lifestyle, you will notice that your body regulates food much better, as it is getting the room to digest everything you ingest, and fasting will get less and less adverse and much more palatable. Much like every other discipline out there—from bodily disciplines, like jogging and working out, to spiritual ones, like praying and reading the Word—fasting will be a science before it's an art. It will be endurance before it's enjoyable, and just like every other habit, vice, and virtue, it will ultimately become supremely enjoyable and your body will feel off if you go extended periods without fasting. Intermittent fasting is the gateway to that enjoyment.

Piggybacking off that last point, I cannot stress enough the sanctity of our physiology. When we eat, sleep, and exercise better, we find that our bodily processes are optimized, and that turbulence period at the onset of the fast becomes almost nonexistent. That brings fasting down to being much more a practice than an isolated event. God desires and created us for communion, and communion is an ongoing relational dynamic. So when our bodies are optimized for the call, we prove ourselves to be good stewards of our health. That's primarily all fasting is about: stewardship. It's the celestial modality of credit through which God entrusts us with more. Health, wealth, and happiness are the irrevocable rewards of good stewardship. My hope in all this is that you would see fasting not as some once-in-a-blue-moon adverse event to be dreaded and endured but rather as a thread being interwoven in every practice, discipline, and aspect of our tripartite nature.

Fasting in Community

The Bible is packed with profound testimonies of personal breakthrough wrought by God's mighty hand, with Him having been moved to mighty acts by the humble entreaties of His fasted children. And many of those acts were brought about through the power of corporate, communal, or national fasts—the "solemn assembly," as Joel 1:14 puts it (ESV). Although powerful and transformative enough as a solo devotional discipline, fasting was created, like prayer and every other meaningful practice, to compound in community. That is how most African, Middle Eastern, Latin, and even Asian cultures do it. That's how Jews in Yom Kippur or even Islamics in Ramadan practice fasting, and that's why the Bible is full of incredible testimonies of communal fasting. Here's a partial list of some of the communal fasts in Scripture:

- The Fast at Mizpah (where the Israelites fasted and repented after their defeat by the Philistines)—1 Samuel 7:5–6
- The Day of Atonement (Yom Kippur)—Leviticus 16:29–31; 23:27–32; Numbers 29:7–11
- The Fast of Esther—Esther 4:15–17

- The Fast of the Fifth Month (commemorating the destruction of the temple)—Zechariah 7:3–5
- The Fast of the Tenth Month (commemorating the siege of Jerusalem)—Zechariah 8:19
- The Fast of Jehoshaphat—2 Chronicles 20:1–4
- The Fast of Ezra—Ezra 8:21–23
- The Fast of Nehemiah—Nehemiah 9:1–3
- The Fast of Joel—Joel 1:14; 2:12–17
- The Fast of Nineveh—Jonah 3:5–9
- The Fast of Daniel—Daniel 9:3–19

The object of all those incredible narratives is to raise a fasting community. I cannot stress that enough. In my personal conversations and casual observance, I have found with startling accuracy that the people who made annual fasts a beautiful practice were the people who formed a supportive community. That is simply the way of mankind. We are a communal people, made in the image of a God who has always existed in community of the Trinity.

When we undertake something communally, the sense of ownership is next-level. When we make fasting communal, we make it a communal value, and when done enough times, it morphs into a cultural value. And at that point, our language changes; instead of, "We are fasting," it becomes, "We are fasters." Fasting then becomes not what we do but who we are. We see this numerous times when a value is celebrated, propagated, and protected within a community, it becomes a defining trait. We look at churches that practice communal prayer and say that's a "praying" church, or a "teaching" church, and so forth. Our church, Saddleback, had a recent challenge in that we are a church that reads, loves, and preaches the Bible, but many of our new people were not familiar with the Bible. Our executive pastor of ministries, Jason Williams, had the answer. He suggested a challenge: "Let's read the entire New Testament in eight weeks as a community."

We gave Bibles away and even had a teaching team available to sit on panels and answer Scripture questions. The result was the most powerful and compelling campaign I have ever been a part of. We gave away 28,000 Bibles to members of our community. We had more than 2,455 Bible book clubs reading the Word. Our on-campus Bible book clubs were attended by 5,500 new people. About 9,800 people participated in the Saddleback Church app, in four different languages, and 444,000 hours were spent in God's Word over that eight-week period! As Pastor Andy pointed out, that was almost 27 million minutes spent in God's Word! Talk about impact! I can't even begin to speak on the stories and all the qualitative metrics that underscored the success of this initiative. Something difficult was made simple because we faced it with friends. That's the exponential power of tapping into community.

I have broken many a personal fast in my lifetime, but I cannot remember a single corporate or communal fast that I didn't see through till the end. A communal commitment mandates a totally different mindset altogether. We can endure so much more if we know that other people are going through the same thing and will be at the finish line to celebrate with us.

My point is that whenever you want to engage in an extended fast, find a community of people to go into it with you. You may be thinking, *But I'm struggling to keep this one friend I have. Where on earth am I going to get this village you speak of?* Trying a local church group can be a very effective method. My wife and I have used social media to invite people to join our fasts. We reached out, mentioned we were fasting, and asked friends, relatives, and total strangers to journey with us. We jumped on Instagram Live every day and processed what we were feeling and hearing. We were quite surprised at the response, and you will be too, I'm sure.

You might remember Matthew 6:18, where Jesus talks about the importance of fasting in secret. While it's a good point, in the context of that particular verse, Jesus was not necessarily placing a value on secrecy; He was speaking out against the desire to be seen and applauded by men for spiritual undertakings rather than seeking God's approval first and foremost. The heart-itude of humility in fasting is more important than the actual act. A sinful, self-promoting attitude becomes the first casualty of a humble, communal fast.

So for the communal, spiritual accountability and also the physical health benefits of having numerous sets of eyes on your physiological process and consequent progress, reach out and form a fasting community. You won't regret it.

Grace and Prayer

Finally, however you choose to incorporate fasting into your lifestyle, seek God's grace! That's the secret weapon. I usually pray the wimpiest prayers before I fast, but thanks to grace and extensive research on fasting, I've found that even the language of my prayers has grown and matured over time. I will pray prayers such as, "Lord, please let ketosis kick in at the end of day one instead of three," and, "Lord, please deepen the impact of autophagy and let no cancerous growths remain." I pray, "Lord, please no headaches or nausea, and please mitigate the discomfort," and you know what? His grace always meets me. Even though the effects and processes are felt physiologically, much like prayer and worship, fasting is still primarily a spiritual exercise, and God's grace can carry you straight to the finish line. So take copious amounts of it—you will need it.

At the end of the day, it takes intention, discipline, and grace to make any spiritual practice a constant. The apostle Peter reminds us, "His divine power has given to us all things that pertain to life and godliness, through the knowledge of Him who called us by glory and virtue" (2 Peter 1:3).

The simple, unassuming, easily ignored, and frequently dismissed practice of fasting changed my entire life. It opened up realms of possibility I never imagined. In the folds of fasting, I witnessed the impossible become possible and the rare become reality. I saw the wild fluctuations in my mindfulness and mental health become anchored in a grounded peace and sublime joy that had always been, up to that point, circumstantial. I saw my body shed pounds upon pounds and morph into a younger-looking, more agile, and healthier version of myself. This simple practice of restraint and consecration ministered to my holistic, tripartite being at every level and transformed me into the believer in it I am today. Nothing else, no other practice I know, spiritual or otherwise, is as transformational. Will it suck? Yes. Is it hard? Absolutely! But when is true transformation ever not? From the caterpillar's cocoon to rehab wards to gyms all around the world, true transformation is always born from the crucible of intense pain and true discomfort. That's what a maternal delivery room is: a liminal space, a painful passageway where the old becomes new. All things worth having are hard to attain, but maybe it's time we, as a people, learn to find the holy in the hard. It will be inconvenient, it will be uncomfortable, but no amount of pain can hold a candle to the incredible transformation that awaits not even at the end but in the middle of this journey. Just say yes and start.

I believe that fasting is a beautiful and potent tool for redemption. Through it, I and many others have reclaimed our health, happiness, and holiness. I have yet to meet anyone who did fasting the way it was designed who was not radically transformed by this incredible practice. The Word, science, and countless testimonies guarantee it.

Fasting saved my life, fasting saved my brother's life, and

prayer and fasting saved my sister's life. That is what I hope this book will be to you: a testimony that points to your impending transformation and the redemption of all you love and may have lost. My zeal for fasting is absolute, and my prayer is that the Lord will restore it into the hands of the church and that through this transformational practice, my generation and the generations after it will once again learn how to fast.

Essential Questions and Answers

IN THE NUMEROUS WORKSHOPS, lectures, and classes I've given on the topic of fasting, I've answered many questions. I've listed them here for you—some quite detailed and others as general guidance—to support your unique fasting journey.

What is a water fast?

A water fast is where you abstain from all food and drink except water. It is often undertaken for health, spiritual, or religious reasons. The duration can vary from twenty-four hours to many days.

What is the difference between intermittent fasting and water fasting?

Intermittent fasting involves alternating periods of eating and fasting (for example, fasting for sixteen hours and eating during an eight-hour window). Water fasting, however, is continuous abstention from all food and calorie-containing drinks for a period, consuming water only. Unless otherwise stated (see Daniel 10:3), the fasting mentioned in the Bible is water fasting.

Is water fasting safe for everyone?

While fasting, in its many iterations, is not only safe but also recommended for everyone, extended water fasting, unfortunately, is not. It's generally not recommended for children, pregnant or breastfeeding women, or people with certain health conditions, such as diabetes, eating disorders, heart conditions, or kidney disease. Even healthy individuals should approach water fasting cautiously and ideally under medical supervision. Determining if water fasting is suitable involves considering your physical health, medical history, and goals. Consultation with a healthcare professional is essential, especially if you have any underlying health conditions or are taking medication. Individual health objectives and personal tolerance to fasting should guide the decision.

Is it safe to water fast without supervision?

Yes for most healthy individuals, even though my recommendation is to fast in community, which is how I believe many kingdom practices should be experienced. Short-term water fasting (twenty-four to seventy-two hours) can be safe when done independently. However, longer fasts or fasting for individuals with preexisting health conditions, the elderly, or those on medication should ideally be done under medical supervision. This is in order to look for and manage potential complications, such as electrolyte imbalances and hypoglycemia, and ensure overall safety.

How do I prepare for a water fast?

> Fasting is more about replacing than it is about abstaining—replacing normal activities with focused times of prayer and feeding on the Word of God.
>
> —Gary Rohrmayer, *Twenty-One Days of Prayer and Fasting*

Physical preparation should start a few days before the fast. Gradually reduce the intake of sugar, caffeine, and processed foods. Increase your hydration and start shifting toward lighter meals, such as salads and soups. Ensure you're in a good state of health and consult a healthcare professional, especially if you have any medical conditions or take medications.

Likewise, spiritual preparation should begin the moment you feel the invitation or burden to fast or make the resolution. As with the physical, don't binge-watch or binge-eat before the onset of the fast, but begin to humbly yield your heart and internally prepare yourself through a shift in your entertainment. I usually start by curating a more muted, introspective worship-music playlist. I then prepare a meeting place or sacred place that I designate for most of my prayer and reading. I got this inspiration from the tent of meeting that was in the center of the children of Israel's camp, and I have found it a most grounding act. I usually pick a secluded space, away from the main thoroughfare, and set the right ambience. This doesn't have to be anything fancy. I have literally temporarily cleared out and used closets and corners for fasting preparation. I make it a no-phone zone, and my family knows to enter that space only to either be part of my worship and prayer or get my attention for an emergency. Everything else can wait.

Finally, mindset is everything. Tell yourself you will see the fast through, and set your face like flint and commit to enduring the entirety of the time God has called you to fast.

How can I track my progress during a water fast?

Progress during a water fast can be tracked through various means: measuring body weight, noting changes in physical appearance, and monitoring energy levels and mental clarity. For health-specific goals, medical tests for blood-glucose or cholesterol levels before and after the fast can provide objective measures of progress. I have also found it incredibly beneficial to keep a fasting journal chronicling everything I'm feeling, thinking, and going though during the fast. After three or four extended water fasts, you begin to see patterns in timelines, how your body responds, and how the Lord primarily speaks to you. This data helps you chart future fasts with efficiency. This personal history with God can inform and inspire your faith journey quite significantly.

What are the stages of water fasting?

The stages of water fasting typically include the following:

1. Initial hunger phase (first one or two days): characterized by strong hunger pangs and intense cravings, among other detox discomforts.

2. Ketosis (usually starts around day two or three): the body begins using ketones for energy, causing hunger to decrease.
3. Deep fasting state (after day three or four): characterized by enhanced autophagy, stable energy levels, and mental clarity.
4. Breaking the fast: requires gradual reintroduction of food.

What should I expect during the first twenty-four hours of water fasting?

What your body does and what you consequently feel the first few days of a fast will always vary based on your dietary habits leading up to the fast. The less healthy and more indulgent you've been eating, the more adverse the effects as your body detoxes or as you suffer withdrawals. So you might experience nothing adverse at all during the first twenty-four hours or maybe just have normal hunger pangs or food cravings. On the other hand, you might experience severe headaches, cramps, mood swings, or irritability, often due to sugar and caffeine withdrawal. Energy levels might fluctuate, and some people feel a sense of heightened alertness, while others feel a bit sluggish. Once again, these are typical symptoms but they will always vary based on each individual's dietary patterns.

Will I experience hunger throughout the entire fast?

No! And that's the beautiful part. Our bodies and our minds assume—and the Enemy likes for us to believe—that if I'm hungry after three hours, I'll surely be *starving* after three days—a logical extrapolation. Hunger is most intense during the first few days of a fast. But as the body adapts to fasting and switches to burning fat for energy, hunger often diminishes. Many people report a significant decrease in hunger after the first two or three days.

Ghrelin is a hormone produced primarily by the stomach that stimulates appetite, increases food intake, and promotes fat storage. During a fast, ghrelin production and its effects on hunger and appetite change over time. In the early stages of fasting (within the first twenty-four to forty-eight hours), ghrelin levels typically increase, which is why people often feel hungry at the beginning of a fast. That increase in ghrelin is a normal physiological response to the absence of food, as the body is signaling a need for nourishment. It is basically the body sending its messenger (ghrelin) to knock on your door and say, *Hey, we need more food to burn for energy and store up for a rainy day.*

Remember, as we covered earlier in the book, the body uses hormones and neurotransmitters to initiate and end physiological processes. However, as the fast progresses, ghrelin levels gradually decline and eventually stabilize at a lower level. That process is known as ghrelin adaptation, or ghrelin resistance. It is essentially the body saying, *Okay, we have a new fuel source. Everything is humming along as it should. No need to panic.* Ketones are also hunger suppressants and mitigate the body's need to release ghrelin.

What are ketones, and how are they related to water fasting?

Great question! We have heard it said that when the body is hungry, it burns fat for fuel, and that propagates weight loss.

While this is technically true, it's an oversimplification. During periods of low food intake, the body cannot synthesize fat and use it for fuel, so it releases fatty acids and sends them to the liver, which breaks them down and converts them into soluble sources of molecular fuel called ketones. They serve as an alternative energy source for the brain and other organs when glucose is scarce. Water fasting accelerates the process of ketosis, where the body primarily uses ketones for energy. It would be a happier world if the body stored reserve energy as ready-made ketones instead of fat, but then the ketones would be synthesized, as they are a preferable energy source to the body. So they are stored, locked up as fat deposits, until there are significant insulin drops and ketosis can begin. I love God's ingenious design of our bodies.

What is autophagy?

> In a fast, the body tears down its defective parts and then builds anew when eating is resumed.
>
> —Herbert M. Shelton, *Fasting for Renewal of Life*

Autophagy is a natural cellular process where cells break down and recycle damaged and dysfunctional components. Water fasting is believed to accelerate autophagy, as the absence of incoming nutrients forces cells to more aggressively clean house and recycle materials. This process is linked to cellular health, longevity, and the prevention of various diseases.

How does water fasting affect electrolyte balance?

Water fasting can disrupt electrolyte balance, particularly in extended fasts. Key electrolytes such as sodium, potassium, and magnesium may become depleted, leading to symptoms like cramps, headaches, and irregular heartbeats. Monitoring and, in some cases, supplementing electrolytes can be important for prolonged fasts.

How does water fasting affect the digestive system?

Water fasting gives the digestive system a rest, which is beneficial for the reproduction and repair of cells within the digestive tract. This respite is especially beneficial for people with certain digestive issues. However, prolonged fasting can also lead to decreased digestive-enzyme production and changes in gut microbiota. Resuming normal eating should be done gradually to avoid gastrointestinal distress.

How long can I safely do a water fast?

The safe duration of a water fast varies by individual. A general guideline for a healthy person ranges from twenty-four to seventy-two hours to fourteen to twenty-one days. Longer fasts (up to forty days) are possible under medical supervision. Factors like hydration levels, individual metabolism, and pre-existing health conditions play crucial roles in determining safe duration.

How often can I do a water fast?

The frequency of your water fasts should be based on individual health goals and physical response. Some people might undertake a short water fast once a month, while others may do it less frequently. Extended or frequent fasting should be approached with caution and ideally under the umbrella of communal accountability and medical supervision.

Is there an optimal time of year to do a water fast?

Fasting is primarily an initiation on our end or a response to a divine invitation from the Lord. Sometimes the Lord calls us to a fast, sometimes our pastors and spiritual leaders will consecrate a fast or call a solemn assembly (see Joel 1:14), and sometimes we engage in a fast to cleanse sluggish, saturated souls or humble ourselves as we attract heaven to intervene on our behalf. Because of this, from a spiritual level, there is no ideal time to fast. I always choose strategic times, such as weekends that blend into holidays, as I can shut myself in and focus on consecration, prayer, and the Word as I fast. The optimal time for a water fast will always depend on individual preferences and lifestyle. From a physiological standpoint, some people find it easier to fast during warmer months due to a naturally decreased appetite, while others prefer colder months when the social demand for outdoor and social activity is not as rampant as in the summer, and they can rest more. It's also important to consider personal schedules and choose a time when you can reduce physical and mental stress.

What are the psychological effects of water fasting?

The greatest battle and the most adverse struggle during fasting will always occur in your mind. At first your body reacts adversely to the lack of caloric intake in the form of food. You feel hunger as the hunger hormone, ghrelin, is released. You feel stomach cramps and physical weakness as your body tries to kick-start you back into habitual eating as a survival mechanism. If you remain steadfast and don't eat, that survival mechanism jump-starts ketosis, autophagy, and all the other fasting-centric processes, and your body relaxes into the routine. But the battle hasn't even truly begun. Your mind then begins acute warfare as it conjures up arguments, excuses, and justifications for you to resume eating. For me, days five to eight are often the most intense. I have found communal accountability or fasting with someone to be irreplaceable. In *The Complete Guide to Fasting*, Dr. Jason Fung wrote,

> Interestingly, I've seen the highest success rates with husbands and wives who try fasting together: the mutual support is a big help and makes fasting far easier.[1]

The most challenging trick the mind will employ during your fast is to cause you to remember in vivid detail every calorically dense food you've ever eaten. You remember the smell of every burger you've ever walked past. Every food ad becomes a serious enticement as the mind employs memories to try to get you to eat. It's a brilliant psychological mechanism for reengagement. The funny thing is that no matter how healthy and habitual your culinary diet was, you will never crave a salad in this phase of the fast. It's always the pizzas, burgers, doughnuts, and shakes that give you the shakes, proving once again that it's psychological enticement. Mahatma Gandhi, in his autobiography, wrote,

> If physical fasting is not accompanied by mental fasting, it is bound to end in hypocrisy and disaster.[2]

Psychologically, fasting can be both challenging and rewarding. It may lead to increased self-awareness, a sense of accomplishment, and a different perspective on hunger and satiety. However, it can also be mentally challenging, triggering food obsessions, irritability, or a sense of deprivation. The psychological impact varies greatly among individuals.

How much water should I drink during a fast?

The general guideline is to drink water according to thirst, which for most people will be around two to three liters per day. I would, however, recommend adding a liter or two to factor in detoxing. Fasting is a dirty process, and I have found that the more water you consume and pass, the less toxins that stay in your body, and poisons and toxins are what cause a lot of the discomforts, like headaches, when we fast. I have had fasts where I drank less water and some more, and the more-water fasts have been smoother for the most part. I recommend drinking more on the front end of the fast because as the fast progresses and the body is optimized, it begins to reject water intake and you will find less motivation to hydrate as the fast prolongs. It is also possible to over-hydrate, so navigate with care. Both dehydration and over-hydration are not advised.

What kind of water is best to drink during a fast?

During a water fast, it's important to drink clean, safe water. Filtered water is often recommended to remove any impurities or contaminants. Some people prefer mineral water to ensure they are getting some electrolytes, but distilled or tap water is generally acceptable if it's of good quality.

Is carbonated water acceptable during a water fast?

I knew the Topo Chico fans would get their day in court! Carbonated water without any added sugars or flavors is generally acceptable during a water fast. It can provide a sense of variety and may help with feelings of hunger. However, it's important to ensure that the carbonated water is free of calories and artificial additives. I personally have found that any variable to regular water upsets my stomach and throws off my flow, but many people use carbonated water and it has worked great with their fasting.

How does water fasting compare to juice fasting?

Because juices almost always contain fructose (also known as fruit sugar and is a type of simple sugar, or monosaccharide, found mostly in fruits), like most carbohydrates, they will always kick you out of ketosis, or a fasted state. That is because the body's metabolic process will always take the path of least resistance and preferentially use the fructose for energy, reducing the need to break down fat into ketones and therefore disrupting the process of ketosis. Anything that raises your insulin levels will cause a disruption to this process and a reset of your body's fasting clock. Water fasting involves consuming only water, which leads to deeper ketosis and potentially more significant autophagy compared to juice fasting. Juice fasting allows for some caloric and nutrient intake, which, though making it easier for some people, doesn't induce the same level of metabolic changes as water fasting. I find going cold turkey easier, though, so my mind can completely switch off food and I can feast on the divine.

Can I drink black coffee or tea during a water fast?

More than any other Discipline, fasting reveals the things that control us.

—Richard Foster, *Celebration of Discipline*

This question introduces an interesting dichotomy, which I believe is perfectly framed by the apostle Paul in 1 Corinthians 10:23, where he reminds us that all things are permissible but not all things are beneficial. Although coffee does not disrupt or take away from the fasting process (as it contains no sugar to kick you out of a fasted, or ketogenic, state), I believe it undercuts a most important benefit: freedom from caffeine addiction. There is nothing more powerful than leaving an extended water fast shackled only to the Lord and His will. I fast for myriad reasons and benefits, but anytime I feel that something has mastery over me, fasting is the antidote. Can you start a morning or function without coffee? Does coffee dictate your mood? If so, then it has mastery over you and should be slain on the altar of fasting. Although I and most purists would argue that a true water fast includes water only, some fasting protocols allow for noncaloric beverages like black coffee and tea. Although these can help suppress appetite, they may also stimulate digestion or have diuretic effects so should be consumed mindfully.

Is dry fasting more effective than water fasting?

The only times I've engaged in a dry fast (abstaining from both food and water) was when I felt as though the Lord was specifically calling me to it, and I have never done a dry fast for longer than three days, nor would I recommend doing so. That is primarily because as your body cleanses itself, it releases many toxins in your body and needs ample amounts of water to flush them out. When dry fasting, I could feel the toxicity of my body, and the weakness, headaches, cramps, and brain fog became almost unbearable. Medical professionals and dieticians alike consider that type of fasting more extreme and potentially dangerous due to the toxicity and the increased risk of dehydration. There is little scientific evidence to suggest it's more effective than water fasting. Water fasting is generally safer and more sustainable, especially for longer durations. I did see incredible breakthrough, though, the few times I did a dry fast, but I also attain good results when I water fast for longer periods, so I can't authoritatively speak to the potency or efficacy of one type of fast over the other. My take is this: If the Lord calls you to it, the reward is in the obedience. So, unless called to it, I wouldn't recommend initiating it, due to the multiple downsides.

How do I know I'm getting enough electrolytes during a water fast?

Maintaining electrolyte balance is crucial. Signs of imbalance include muscle cramps, weakness, and headaches. To prevent that, some people choose to supplement with electrolytes (sodium, potassium, magnesium) in their water, especially during extended fasts. Electrolytes do not break your fast and should be taken if those symptoms persevere beyond twenty-four hours. However, the decision to supplement should be based on individual health needs and, if possible, under the accountability of your fasting community and the guidance of a healthcare professional.

What are the signs of successful water fasting?

Success in water fasting can be subjective and varies depending on personal goals. Common signs include achieving desired outcomes like weight loss, improved mental clarity, and enhanced physical and mental well-being, or achieving specific health goals like better blood-sugar control. Feeling a sense of accomplishment and not experiencing severe negative side effects can also indicate a successful fast. Some of the spiritual signs could be peace, inner clarity, answered prayer, spiritual grounding, discipline, and a more intimate and meaningful walk with the Lord. We will always find growth and gain simultaneously across our spirits, souls, and bodies if we look.

What are the benefits of water fasting?

There are physical, spiritual, and psychological benefits to fasting. The majority were covered in the first part of the book. A few potential physical benefits include weight loss, improved insulin sensitivity, enhanced cellular-repair processes (autophagy), reduced inflammation, and a possible decrease in the risk factors for chronic diseases. A few soul benefits include mental clarity and emotional detoxification. Remember, the evidence varies with every individual. Not all benefits are universally experienced.

Are there any long-term effects of water fasting?

We know the answer to be affirmative in the spiritual, and extensive personal testimonies attest to the fact, but the long-term effects of water fasting are not well studied from scientific or medical perspectives. Although short-term benefits like weight loss and improved metabolic markers are documented, the long-term impact on health, especially from repeated or prolonged fasts, requires more research.

Can water fasting contribute to a longer lifespan?

Research, particularly in animal models, suggests that calorie restriction, including fasting, may have lifespan-extending effects, possibly by reducing metabolic stress and enhancing cellular-repair mechanisms. However, direct evidence in humans is limited, and it's unclear whether the benefits observed in animal studies fully translate to humans. Moreover, the potential longevity benefits of fasting must be balanced against risks and quality-of-life considerations.

Will I lose weight during a water fast?

Absolutely! Water fasting typically leads to weight loss due to a significant reduction in calorie intake. Initially, much of the weight lost is water weight and glycogen (stored carbohydrates), but with prolonged fasting, the body begins to burn fat for energy. However, some weight might be regained once normal eating is resumed. A metabolic complication called refeeding syndrome can occur when a person who has been in a state of starvation or prolonged fasting begins to eat again. It is characterized by severe electrolyte imbalances and fluid shifts within the body, which can lead to serious complications. That is why it is incredibly important to break the fast the right way, and we will answer how as a separate question in this section.

Will water fasting help with skin conditions?

Varied testimonies and anecdotal evidence suggest that water fasting improves skin conditions like acne and eczema, potentially due to reduced inflammation and the autophagic process. There is a noticeable glow of the skin as the body finishes the detoxing process, allowing all nutrients to reach the skin. Most people having done extended fasts testify to this. However, scientific research in this area is limited, and only dermatologists can definitively say whether it does or does not happen. It would be helpful for individuals with skin conditions to consult a dermatologist before undertaking a water fast and after for the record.

Can fasting help with allergies?

Personal testimony and anecdotal reports suggest that fasting may help alleviate allergy symptoms in some individuals, possibly due to reduced inflammation and a reset of the immune response.

Can fasting improve my immune system?

There is significant evidence to suggest that fasting, particularly short-term or intermittent, can rejuvenate the immune system by promoting the turnover of immune cells and reducing inflammation. Extended water fasting, however, might temporarily weaken the immune system due to nutrient deficiencies for the duration of the fast.

Can water fasting be beneficial for lymphatic health?

The idea that water fasting can benefit lymphatic health is based on the theory that fasting can reduce inflammation and stimulate autophagy, which might help the lymphatic system function more effectively. Although that is still a theory, there is some validity. Maintaining hydration during fasting is crucial for overall lymphatic and bodily functions.

Can water fasting help with inflammation?

Water fasting can reduce inflammation by decreasing the pro-duction of pro-inflammatory cytokines and increasing anti-inflammatory cytokines. Cytokines are small proteins that help regulate inflammation and also control the activity and growth of blood cells and other immune system cells. They also signal the immune system's response to germs or other harmful substances. That positive effect is part of why fasting is thought to be beneficial for certain chronic inflammatory conditions.

Can water fasting help with autoimmune and inflammatory diseases?

There's some evidence that fasting can modulate the immune system and benefit autoimmune conditions by reducing in-flammation. However, the research is still emerging, and indi-viduals with autoimmune diseases should approach fasting cautiously and under medical supervision, as fasting can also stress the body and exacerbate symptoms.

Can water fasting improve cognitive function?

Absolutely! It is one of the primary markers of an effective fast. Improved focus and cognitive clarity kick in once the initial turbulence phase passes, possibly due to increased production of ketones, which can be efficient fuel sources for the brain. However, the timeline for those effects is not universal, and some people may experience decreased concentration or brain fog, especially during the initial stages of fasting, before the clarity occurs. In the words of my fellow teaching pastor, Stacie Wood, "Trust the process."

Can water fasting improve joint health?

Some individuals report relief from joint pain and improvement in conditions like arthritis during and after water fasting, potentially due to reduced inflammation. However, those effects are typically short-term, and fasting should not be seen as a substitute for medical treatment for joint diseases. More research is needed to understand the long-term impact of fasting on joint health.

Can water fasting regulate blood-sugar levels?

Yes! Water fasting can significantly lower blood-sugar levels as the body uses up glucose stores and transitions to burning fat for energy. This can improve insulin sensitivity and be beneficial for people with type 2 diabetes or metabolic syndrome. It's always crucial for individuals with blood-sugar issues, especially those on insulin or other glucose-lowering medications, to monitor their levels closely mid-fast and keep a healthcare provider's number handy on their phone, as there is a risk of hypoglycemia (abnormal decrease of sugar in the blood).

Can water fasting balance hormones?

Water fasting can affect various hormones, including insulin, ghrelin (the hunger hormone), and leptin (the satiety hormone). These changes can lead to improved insulin sensitivity and alterations in hunger and fullness cues. However, the effects on other hormones, such as sex hormones, are more complex and can vary. I always recommend fasting whenever someone has a hormonal imbalance, though, and every case I've recommended has seen significant improvement. Remember, the whole process and principle of fasting is based on the garden work in Genesis: bringing all things to rest and equilibrium so the work of cleansing and creation can begin. Once again, if there is any medical problem, take it to the Lord when you fast and contend for your healing in faith. God unabashedly invites us to engage Him in this way.

Can water fasting help with fertility issues?

I would encourage those dealing with infertility to hold fast to the Word of God, with the clearest promise being found in Exodus 23:26: "None will miscarry or be barren in your land. I will give you a full life span" (NIV). And the divine response? "Behold, I am the LORD, the God of all flesh. Is there anything too hard for Me?" (Jeremiah 32:27). That would be the mountain I would command to move in my prayers as I fast for this issue. The physiological and medical impact of water fasting on fertility, however, is not well understood. Some research suggests that caloric restriction can affect hormone levels and influence fertility, but the effects can be complex and vary among individuals. Women trying to conceive or those with existing fertility issues should be particularly cautious and consult a healthcare provider before attempting a water fast. Because fasting improves the overall health of a man, though, it might be worth it for couples since male health contributes significantly to the health of the placenta and the baby.[3]

How does water fasting affect gut microbiota?

Water fasting can significantly affect gut-microbiota composition. Reduced food intake alters the nutrient landscape in the gut, which can lead to changes in microbial populations. Those changes might contribute to some of the health benefits of fasting, like reduced inflammation, but they might also pose risks, such as reduced microbial diversity.

I have a fast/slow metabolism. Can fasting reset it?

Fasting can temporarily change how your body metabolizes energy, mainly shifting from using glucose to using fat as a fuel source (ketosis). However, that is not a permanent reset. Once normal eating resumes, the body typically returns to its previous metabolic state. Long-term metabolic changes are more effectively achieved through sustained lifestyle changes, including diet and exercise.

Is it possible to gain weight back after water fasting?

Yes, it's common to regain weight after water fasting, especially if you return to previous eating habits. The initial weight loss during a water fast often includes a significant amount of water weight and glycogen, which are quickly regained when you resume eating, particularly if you consume a high-carbohydrate diet.

What are the emotional challenges of water fasting?

Common challenges of water fasting include dealing with hunger, resisting the temptation to eat, feeling isolated or excluded in social settings involving food, and experiencing emotional responses to not eating, such as irritability or mood swings. It can also bring up emotional issues related to food, such as guilt and anxiety.

How will water fasting affect my mood?

Mood changes are common during water fasting. Some people report feeling more clearheaded or emotionally balanced, while others experience irritability, anxiety, or low mood, particularly in the initial stages of fasting. Those changes can be due to fluctuations in blood-sugar levels, withdrawal from certain foods or substances, and psychological factors.

How does water fasting affect sleep?

Fasting can affect sleep patterns in different ways. Some people report improved sleep quality and deeper sleep, while others experience insomnia or disrupted sleep, particularly in the early stages of fasting. I hardly sleep well during fasts, while my wife, Pam, gets her best sleep when fasting. In the end, though, I have found that past the equilibrium point, whether you sleep four hours or eight, it all balances out and your body is optimized so that you always wake up feeling refreshed. The marvels of fasting! This variance can be due to changes in hormones and metabolism.

How does water fasting affect the menstrual cycle?

Water fasting potentially can cause irregularities or missed periods. That is due to changes in energy intake affecting hormonal balance, particularly estrogen and progesterone. However, due to all the internal processes engaged, most cultures do not recommend fasting for pregnant women, so I would once again leave this particular decision to the woman, the Lord, and the woman's ob-gyn. Women with a history of menstrual irregularities or fertility issues should approach fasting cautiously and consult a healthcare provider.

Are there any risks associated with water fasting?

I would categorize most of the risks as the expected risks that could arise with a deep cleanse or cellular detox. The body goes through an intensive spring-clean of sorts, and then all the toxins and garbage need to be removed. Potential risks could include nutrient deficiencies, loss of muscle mass, electrolyte imbalances, and orthostatic hypotension (dizziness upon standing). Water fasting can also exacerbate certain medical conditions like gout and kidney stones.

Can water fasting lead to eating disorders?

While water fasting itself is not a cause of eating disorders, it can trigger disordered eating patterns in susceptible individuals. Those with a history of eating disorders should exercise accountability and caution when contemplating a fast. I subjectively believe God will meet you and can consequently heal you of eating disorders in a fast, but it's crucial to approach fasting with communal accountability and a healthy mindset and to prioritize overall well-being over extreme weight loss.

Will I experience headaches during a water fast?

Almost always! Headaches are a common side effect during the initial stages of water fasting, often due to dehydration, withdrawal from caffeine, or the body adjusting to ketosis. Staying well hydrated and easing into the fast by reducing caffeine intake beforehand can help mitigate this.

Will I lose muscle during my water fast?

To minimize muscle loss during a water fast, it's important to avoid strenuous exercise, as the body cannot adequately repair and build muscle without protein intake. Keeping hydrated and ensuring adequate electrolyte balance can also help. However, some muscle loss during extended fasting is almost inevitable as the body eventually utilizes amino acids for energy.

Is it normal to experience dizziness during a water fast?

Dizziness can occur during a water fast, often due to low blood sugar or dehydration. It's important to drink enough water and get up slowly from sitting or lying-down positions to prevent lightheadedness. If dizziness is severe or persistent, it's a sign to end the fast and seek medical advice.

Is it normal to feel cold during a water fast?

Feeling cold is a common experience during water fasting, as food intake helps generate internal body heat. Reduced calorie consumption can lower the metabolic rate, leading to a decreased production of body heat. That was the biggest challenge for me when I went past day ten in water fasting. The temperature could be turned way up but my extremities, especially my feet, would be frigid. That would severely affect my quality of sleep and throw off my days completely until I discovered a solution: hot water bottles! Yep, that's it. Good ole hot water bottles. Heat up water in a kettle, pour it into the bottle, and use the bottle to warm your feet as you sleep, rest, or work. Water bottles run from about six dollars on Amazon to about thirty for the fancy ones.

What precautions should seniors take when water fasting?

Although there are extensive case studies of people (my father included) who water fasted well into their eighties and maintained relatively healthy and active lifestyles, I would still use caution in recommending water fasting to anyone over age sixty. Age-related physiological changes such as decreased kidney function, altered metabolic rates, and medication interactions make fasting riskier. Seniors should fast only under medical supervision and might be advised to consider milder forms of fasting, like intermittent fasting, which can be safer and more suitable.

Will water fasting give me bad breath?

Absolutely! Bad breath, or halitosis, will most likely occur during water fasting, primarily due to the production of ketones, especially acetone, which is released in the breath. That is a common side effect of ketosis and is often referred to as "keto breath." The toxins being expelled from your body also gather on the tongue, giving it a weird color and a bad odor.

Can I chew gum or suck on mints for bad breath during a fast?

I wouldn't recommend it. You don't want the sugar in your gum kicking you out of a fasted/ketogenic state. I'm even wary of using sugar-free gum simply because it has other ingredients I'd rather not introduce into my body in its vulnerable state of detox. My advice and recommendation? Mouthwash! It's safe and I've found it highly effective. I carry a little travel-size mouthwash in my pocket and before I get around people, I usually go to the bathroom and gargle. In addition to better breath, I find the little bite refreshing to my dry mouth. Another option would be to plan your fast around times when you know you won't have to go out in public.

Can athletes fast before or during a competition?

Although I have athlete friends who would fast during competition days and have reported optimal performance during the competition, athletes require significant energy and nutrient intake for performance and recovery, so water fasting might not be suitable, especially during training or competition periods. I would recommend this decision being at the discretion of the athlete and their mandate from the Lord for that particular fast. Sometimes the Lord calls us to sacrificially do things that don't necessarily align with conventional wisdom, and the results and rewards of that obedience far outweigh the reservations of good counsel. Athletes interested in fasting should consult with a sports nutritionist and consider timing the fast during off-seasons or rest periods.

Can I exercise while on a water fast?

I have had two groups of people ask me this. The first group are the people who understand and are allured by the benefits of fasting and want to double up on the benefits and help the process along. The second are habitual exercisers who believe that the sedentary nature of fasting will disrupt their routine.

To the first group, sure! Light exercise such as walking and gentle stretching may be okay, but intense physical activity is not recommended. During a fast, the body's energy levels are lower, and exercising strenuously can lead to fatigue, light-headedness, or muscle breakdown. It's important to listen to your body and adjust activity levels accordingly.

To the second group, I always advise to first consider your primary drivers. In fasting, the motive and heart posture are as important as the physical benefits. Is your body an idol that needs its fitness fix? Let the Holy Spirit search your intents and motives, and respond as He leads.

Can I take prescription medications while water fasting?

Whether you can continue taking prescription medications during a water fast depends on the medication and your individual health situation. Some medications require food intake for proper absorption or to prevent gastrointestinal irritation. Always consult with a healthcare provider before fasting if you're on medication, as adjustments may be necessary.

Can I take vitamins and supplements while water fasting?

Opinions vary on taking supplements during a water fast. I would subjectively suggest that it's best to avoid anything but water to allow the body to fully engage in the fasting process. That is how people did it in the Bible, and that is how I've seen the most results when I've done it. Remember, fasting is a process that was baked into our design when heaven perfected our blueprint. Other people recommend basic supplements like multivitamins, electrolytes, and magnesium to prevent deficiencies, especially during longer fasts. I don't trust the purity of the ingredients or even the accuracy of the labels on most multivitamins, and the last thing I want to do is introduce more external variables into such an intimate bodily process. My advice is to let the body do what it was designed to do. I would, however, recommend taking electrolytes if you are dehydrated or feeling dizzy, as they do not contain sugar and therefore cannot kick you out of a ketogenic, or fasted, state. The final decision should be based on your individual health needs and, ideally, the advice of your primary healthcare provider.

Can I work during a water fast?

I will answer this by using the can-and-should paradigm. Whether you can work during a water fast depends on your physical condition and the nature of your work. Although many people can continue with their usual activities, performing jobs requiring intense physical or mental effort might be more challenging. It's important to listen to your body and not overexert yourself. For first-time fasters, consider starting the fast on a nonwork day to understand how your body reacts to it.

Now, whether you *should* work during your fast is a different story. If possible, schedule fasting during off days or Sabbaths so you can maintain a rested heart posture and spend your time in deep meditative prayer, worship, and the Word. Working while fasting does not mitigate your fast, disqualify you, or make you less spiritual, but I believe taking time to focus solely on your fast, listening to the Lord and your body, gives you a strategic advantage. Because of my meat-heavy diet, I always bake into the front end of my fast what I call a throwaway day, where my body is in a deep state of detox and I just lie in bed and let it do what it does. I'm usually too weak to pray, meditate, or do anything worthwhile while I'm waiting for my body to stabilize.

How do I manage social situations while water fasting?

Navigating social situations while fasting can be challenging. In the cases where social interaction is unavoidable, I've found it helpful to plan ahead—informing friends and family about my fasting or scheduling social gatherings outside of mealtimes. Focusing on the social aspect rather than food, such as engaging in conversation or non-food-related activities, can also help. It's incredibly difficult to be around food and simply rely on our willpower to abstain. Dr. Jason Fung cautions us in this way:

> Try to physically remove yourself from all food stimuli during a fast. Cooking a meal or even just seeing and smell-

ing food while fasting is almost unbearably difficult. This is not simply a matter of weak willpower. Our cephalic phase responses are fully activated, and to feel those responses without actually eating is like trying to stop a piranha feeding frenzy. This, of course, is the same reason you should not shop for food when hungry, or keep snacks in the pantry.[4]

I feel unwell during this water fast. Should I break it?

That depends on the severity of the symptoms. When you fast, you will experience every discomfort imaginable. I want to disenfranchise you of the notion that fasting will be easy. It's quite the contrary. Fasting is an active death. It's a cellular deconstruction and spring-clean from the inside out. It's supposed to be uncomfortable. When we expect an easy fast, we set ourselves up for disappointment. For example, the first day or two may be marked by dizziness, migraines, hunger pains, and stomach cramps. That could be primarily because you're an addict. You're addicted to sugar, you're addicted to caffeine, you're addicted to salts and fats, and there is a severe withdrawal that gets triggered when you don't get your fix. Push through that. You may lose sleep and experience night sweats and shivers. That all happened to me the first time I fasted, but then again, I used to drink two sodas a day and had candy bowls at every workstation. Black tea, which has the highest caffeine concentration of any teas, was also a daily morning and night go-to, so I was a total addict. All in all, the body's process of cleaning you out and the severity of your withdrawal will be determined by your dietary habits pre-fast.

If your symptoms are more acute, such as fainting, heart palpitations, or severe weakness, it's important to stop the fast and seek medical attention. Feeling slightly hungry, having mild headaches, or experiencing a bit of fatigue can be normal, but any severe discomfort is a sign to end the fast. That is why the safest and best way to fast is with communal accountability, with your doctor also aware of your fasting commitment.

What are the warning signs that I should stop a water fast immediately?

Remember, your body is feeling all the symptoms, but fasting is still primarily a spiritual exercise, waged across three fronts (spirit, soul, and body), and all three will experience a degree of discomfort. Immediate cessation of a water fast is advised if you experience fainting, heart palpitations, severe headache, confusion, or any symptom that feels unusually severe or concerning. Those can be signs of serious complications like electrolyte imbalances or dehydration. I cannot stress the importance of perseverance, though. My rule in fasting is to give it a day. If your symptoms are severe, lie down, and if they're more severe the next day, then consult. But like I said, your mind and body will spin up dire narratives to get you to eat. Don't. The nagging feeling usually sorts itself out.

How should I break a water fast?

Breaking a water fast should be done gradually. Start with easily digestible foods like broth, juice, and soft fruits. Over the next few days, slowly reintroduce other foods, starting with small portions. Pay attention to how your body reacts, as digestive sensitivity after a fast is common.

What are the best resources to learn more about water fasting?

Reliable resources for learning about water fasting include scientific journals, books by health and nutrition experts, and reputable health websites. Along with reading this resource and numerous other faith-based books from spiritual thought leaders and luminary thinkers, look for information that includes research and insights from medical professionals. Some suggested authors and experts in the field include Dr. Jason Fung, Dr. Pradip Jamnadas, and Dr. Valter Longo.

Acknowledgments

TO PAM AND SILO, the lioness and the man-cub! I can't think of a better crew to experience where God takes this book and all He does through it. Let's keep turning the pages of the story He has so beautifully written for us. Oh, the places we'll go!

To my father, J. J. Sibanda, and my mother, Rev A. Sibanda, thank you for equipping me and my twelve siblings with everything we ever needed for life and godliness. I'm honored to be your legacy.

To those twelve siblings, I love you all. God couldn't have surrounded me with a better family.

To my parents-in-law, Patrick and Gladys, and to the Mpandes, thank you for all your prayers and patience through this process. I'm blessed to call you family.

To my friend and agent, Tom Dean, and the entire A Drop of Ink family, from meeting in the mountains of Colorado almost a decade ago to birthing this first of many projects, working with you feels like holding hands with a friend. You have turned a daunting process into a truly fun experience. Thank you for speaking value to all that is in me.

To the best editor in the entire world, Estee Zandee, your brilliance, care, and candor throughout this project have been God's generous gift to me. You have breathed life to every iteration of this book and brought a clarity to it that I know God will use to bless so many. Thank you for finding me. Thank you for encouraging me. Thank you for seeing value in my voice. And thank you for birthing this book with me. Writing with your help in the editing process has felt like co-creating with a friend, and my prayer is that this is the first of many.

Laura Barker and my entire Waterbrook and Multnomah family, thank you for bringing me home.

Laura Wright and Cara Iverson, thank you for lending your gifts to this book. You guys are fun!

John Mark Comer, you have been instrumental in shaping my orthopraxy since I first heard the Bridgetown Podcast almost a decade ago. It was also on your podcast that the first domino fell that led to this book. Your love for Jesus, your brilliance, your humility, and your friendship have truly been a gift. I thank the Lord for the gift of you, my friend.

To the ToddFather, Todd Proctor, very few people have had the compounding impact your friendship continues to have on my life. Thank you for blazing a trail worth following. You and Lisa are a gift.

Scott Dawson, running with you and following you has

made me a better husband, follower of Jesus, and sharer of the gospel. Thank you for loving God, people, and your family well enough for all to follow. Your friendship means the world.

Pastor Emmanuel Essien, thank you for modeling integrity and for seeing, cultivating, and platforming the teaching gift in me. You and Mama Emem are incredible role models.

Pastor Andy and Stacie Wood, thank you for loving Jesus *so* well and for inviting us all into it. I love, honor, and am excited to run with you.

Michael and Lorissa Miller, you are a rare gift to this generation and to the Sibandas. Thank you for shaping my hunger, pursuit, leadership, and expression. It's an honor to know you guys. Love you!

To Pastor Jason and Joy Williams, my fellow Texans! You have redeemed the meaning of good pastoring and leadership. Your love for God and for people defines you and has rubbed off on us in the best of ways. Your friendship means the world. Thank you.

Peter and Nanette Slover, you are a blessing to all who cross your paths. The Sibandas love and honor you.

Pastor Chris Sonksen, thank you for the consistent love and investment in every aspect of my leadership. Love you and Laura.

Michael Sieber and the Sieblets, I'm so thankful for your love for God, your family, friendship and leadership. The next bowl of queso is on me!

Michael Chitwood, you're one of the most incredible leaders I've ever met. Thank you for always believing in me.

Brother Corey Russell, you shaped the *fire* inside of me

from the first time I heard your voice. Thank you for helping me orient my life around the flame.

Eric Morgan, the Lions are home. From the first day I walked into your Bible study until today, our hearts still burn when we talk of Him. Love you and Kate so much. Let's build *His* kingdom.

Chuck and Anna Maher, I love you guys so much. Thank you for being the voice the Lord uses to always speak wisdom and counsel into me.

Andreas Kisslinger, from day one, you have been a friend, a brother and a believer in God's call over my life. Here's to laughing through many, many more nights my friend. Love you and Marlene.

To my fearless leaders, Edgar Sandoval, Chris Glynn, Rusty Funk, Steve Spear and the incredible QOT, and Amanda Bowman. Thank you to my entire World Vision family for loving God in the margins, and for giving me the space and platform to change the world with such an incredible organization.

Eula Dillon, everybody needs a friend like you. Thank you for always speaking destiny into me, and for pushing me toward this book for almost twenty years. You're a real one.

Elijah Mwape, very few people are graced with friends and brothers like you. Thank you for always keeping my call and focus front and center.

Pastor Justin Miller—leader, brother, and friend—thank you for always pouring life into me and for doing it with so much fun and joy in the process! The platforms have always been the bonus. Love you. IFOI.

Dr. Will and Dehavilland Ford, from that initial conversation about the Levites, the flame has never gone out. Thank you for almost two decades of love and friendship.

Papa Jerry Haynes, your words have been such a source of comfort, guidance, and blessing. Blessed to call you Pops!

To Jen Moreno: Hey, woman of God, we wrote the book!

Notes

Chapter One: Body, Soul, and Spirit

1. *Ratatouille,* directed by Brad Bird (Burbank, Calif.: Walt Disney Pictures, 2007).

2. Jon Entine, *Abraham's Children: Race, Identity, and the DNA of the Chosen People* (New York: Grand Central Publishing, 2007), 153.

3. Steve Jobs, "It just works. Seamlessly," YouTube video, 1:19, posted by "all about Steve Jobs.com," September 19, 2009, www.youtube.com/watch?v=qmPq00jelpc.

4. Walter Martin, *The Kingdom of the Cults: The Definitive Work on the Subject* (Bloomington, Minn.: Bethany, 2019).

5. James Strong, *Strong's Exhaustive Concordance of the Bible,* #5590, https://biblehub.com/greek/5590.htm.

6. "Environmental Noise Guidelines for the European Region," World Health Organization (WHO), 2018, www.who.int/europe/publications/i/item/9789289053563.

Chapter Two: A Humbled Soul

1. Lesley Hazleton, "The Doubt Essential to Faith," TEDGlobal, June 2013, www.ted.com/talks/lesley_hazleton_the_doubt_essential_to_faith.

2. Geron Davis, "In the Presence of Jehovah," *Holy Ground (Live)*, 2013.

Chapter Three: Making the Impossible Possible

1. Watchman Nee, *The Normal Christian Life* (Carol Stream, Ill.: Tyndale, 1977), 12.
2. Matthew 8:26; 14:31; 16:8; Luke 12:28; see Mark 4:40.

Chapter Four: Foundations

1. 2022 Real Research Survey, "The Popularity of Intermittent Fasting, https://realresearcher.com/media/survey-results-on-the -popularity-of-intermittent-fasting.
2. See Job 31:1.
3. Brother Lawrence, *The Practice of the Presence of God* (New Kensington, Pa.: Whitaker House, 1982), 48.
4. Brother Lawrence, *The Practice of the Presence of God*, 48.
5. Abraham Joshua Heschel, *The Sabbath: Its Meaning for Modern Man* (New York: Farrar, Straus and Giroux, 2005), 13.
6. Heschel, *The Sabbath*, 10.

Chapter Five: The Posture

1. John Adams, "Letter from John Adams to Abigail Adams, Post 12 May 1780," Massachusetts Historical Society, accessed August 1, 2024, www.masshist.org/digitaladams/archive/doc?id= L17800512jasecond.
2. Pete Greig, *Dirty Glory: Go Where Your Best Prayers Take You* (Colorado Springs, Colo.: NavPress, 2016).
3. Pete Greig and Dave Roberts, *Red Moon Rising: Rediscover the Power of Prayer* (Colorado Springs, Colo.: David C Cook, 2015).
4. To learn more about 24-7 Prayer International, visit www.24 -7prayer.com.
5. See James Strong, *Strong's Exhaustive Concordance of the Bible*, #583, https://biblehub.com/hebrew/583.htm.
6. Caroline Cobb, "Would Jesus Turn Over Tables in Today's Church?," The Gospel Coalition, April 29, 2021, www .thegospelcoalition.org/article/jesus-turn-tables-church.

7. Josephus Flavius, *The Works of Josephus: Complete and Un-abridged,* trans. William Whiston (Peabody, Mass.: Hendrickson, 1980). Specifically, the mention of corruption among the high priests and their abuse of power can be found in "Antiquities of the Jews," book 20, chapter 9, section 2.

8. "Jesus Cleanses the Temple," Ligonier Ministries, January 23, 2018, www.ligonier.org/learn/devotionals/jesus-cleanses-the -temple.

Chapter Six: Fasting and Our Physiology

1. Roy A. Wise, "Dual Roles of Dopamine in Food and Drug Seeking: Drive-Reward Paradox," *Biological Psychiatry* 73, no. 9 (October 8, 2012): 819–26, https://doi.org/10.1016/j.biopsych.2012.09.001.

2. Dr. Pradip Jamnadas, "Fasting for Survival Lecture by Dr. Pradip Jamnadas," YouTube video, 1:20:58, posted by "The Galen Foundation," August 16, 2019, www.youtube.com/watch?v= RuOvn4UqznU&t=10s.

3. Marit K. Zinöcker and Inge A. Lindseth, "The Western Diet–Microbiome-Host Interaction and Its Role in Metabolic Disease," *Nutrients* 10, no. 3 (2018): 365, https://doi.org/10.3390/ nu10030365.

4. "NIH Study Shows How Insulin Stimulates Fat Cells to Take in Glucose," National Institutes of Health, September 7, 2010, www .nih.gov/news-events/news-releases/nih-study-shows-how -insulin-stimulates-fat-cells-take-glucose.

5. Gwyneth S. T. Soon and Michael Torbenson, "The Liver and Gly-cogen: In Sickness and Health," *International Journal of Molecular Sciences* 24, no. 7 (2023): 6133, https://pubmed.ncbi.nlm.nih.gov/ 37047105/.

6. Megan E. Capozzi et al., "The Limited Role of Glucagon for Keto-genesis During Fasting or in Response to SGLT2 Inhibition," *Diabetes* 69, no. 5 (May 2020): 882–892, www.ncbi.nlm.nih.gov/pmc/ articles/PMC7171961/.

7. Gal Tsaban et al., "Diet-Induced Fasting Ghrelin Elevation Re-flects the Recovery of Insulin Sensitivity and Visceral Adiposity Regression," *The Journal of Clinical Endocrinology and Metabolism*

107, no. 2 (February 2022): 336–45, https://doi.org/10.1210/clinem/dgab681.

8. Mark P. Mattson et al., "Intermittent Metabolic Switching, Neuro-plasticity and Brain Health," *Nature Reviews Neuroscience* 19 (2018): 81–94, https://doi.org/10.1038/nrn.2017.156.

9. Chia-Wie Cheng et al., "Prolonged Fasting Reduces IGF-1/PKA to Promote Hematopoietic-Stem-Cell-Based Regeneration and Reverse Immunosuppression," *50 Cell Stem Cell* 14, no. 6 (June 5, 2014): 810–23, https://doi.org/10.1016/j.stem.2014.04.014.

Chapter Seven: The Inner Battle

1. Matthew 6:34 (TPT); Cristy Lane, "One Day at a Time," *One Day at a Time: America's Favorite Songs of Faith and Inspiration* (LS Records, 1981).

2. Dr. Myles Munroe, "4 Keys to Fast Effectively with Instant Results," posted February 9, 2019, by Wisdom for Dominion, YouTube, 11 min., 34 sec., www.youtube.com/watch?v=GCb HxUlHZqI.

3. Andrew Murray, *With Christ in the School of Prayer* (The New Christian Classics Library, 2018), 88.

4. Johnson Oatman, Jr., "Count Your Blessings" (1897), public domain.

Chapter Eight: After the Fast

1. Yixuan Fang et al., "Short-Term Intensive Fasting Enhances the Immune Function of Red Blood Cells in Humans," *Immunity and Ageing* 20, no. 44 (August 30, 2023), https://immunityageing.biomedcentral.com/articles/10.1186/s12979-023-00359-3#.

2. See Nassim Nicholas Taleb, *Antifragile: Things That Gain from Disorder* (New York: Random House, 2012), 8.

Essential Questions and Answers

1. Jason Fung, with Jimmy Moore, *The Complete Guide to Fasting: Heal Your Body Through Intermittent, Alternate-Day, and Extended Fasting* (Las Vegas: Victory Belt, 2016), 186.

2. M. K. Gandhi, *An Autobiography or the Story of My Experiments with Truth,* trans. Mahadev Desai (Ahmedabad, India: Navajivan Trust, 1963), 203.

3. Judith Finlayson, "What Men Eat and Drink May Affect Their Babies' Health," *The Washington Post,* October 13, 2019, www .washingtonpost.com/health/what-men-eat-and-drink-may-affect -their-babies-health/2019/10/11/33d4aefa-da42-11e9-bfb1 -849887369476_story.html.

4. Fung, *Complete Guide to Fasting,* 172.

About the Author

Originally from Zimbabwe, **Reward Sibanda** is a speaker, a writer, the teaching pastor at Saddleback Church, and the senior director of national church engagement and ministry partnerships for one of the largest Christian humanitarian organizations in the world, World Vision.

Reward has a fresh and unique perspective that challenges conventional thought, stemming from his African upbringing, Ubuntu values, extensive travel, and constant interplay with diverse global cultures. He thrives on empowering people from all ages and walks of life and challenging them to transcend any limitation and pursue God's best for them. This, along with his global philanthropic work and high affinity for thought leadership, is at the core of Reward's mission and values.

Reward also loves curating safe spaces for candid conversations that address some of the world's toughest topics. When not speaking or traveling around the world, he can be found serving at his local church, bent over a good book in his favorite chair, or watching reruns of *Star Trek* and *The West Wing*. Reward currently resides in Southern California with his wife, Pam, and their toddler son, Silo.

About the Type

This book was set in Horley Old Style, a typeface issued by the English type foundry Monotype in 1925. It is an old-style face, with such distinctive features as lightly cupped serifs and an oblique horizontal bar on the lowercase "e."